FOUL DEEDS & SUSPICIOUS
DEATHS AROUND NEWPORT

FOUL DEEDS AND SUSPICIOUS DEATHS Series

Foul Deeds and Suspicious Deaths series explores in detail crimes of passion, brutal murders, grisly deeds and foul misdemeanours. From Victorian street crime, to more modern murder where passion, jealousy, or social depravation brought unexpected violence to those involved. From mysterious death to murder and manslaughter, the books are a fascinating insight into not only those whose lives are forever captured by the suffering they endured, but also into the society that moulded and shaped their lives. Each book takes you on a journey into the darker and unknown side of the area.

Other titles in the series

Foul Deeds and Suspicious Deaths in Blackburn & Hyndburn,
Steve Greenhalgh.
ISBN: 1-903425-18-2   £9.99

Foul Deeds and Suspicious Deaths in and around Chesterfield, Geoffrey Sadler.
ISBN: 1-903425-30-1   £9.99

Foul Deeds and Suspicious Deaths in & around Durham, Maureen Anderson
ISBN: 1-903425-46-8   £9.99

Foul Deeds and Suspicious Deaths in and around Halifax, Stephen Wade
ISBN: 1-903425-45-X   £9.99

Foul Deeds and Suspicious Deaths in Leeds, David Goodman
ISBN: 1-903425-08-5   £9.99

Foul Deeds and Suspicious Deaths in Nottingham, Kevin Turton
ISBN: 1-903425-35-2   £9.99

Foul Deeds and Suspicious Deaths in and around Rotherham, Kevin Turton
ISBN: 1-903425-27-1   £9.99

Foul Deeds and Suspicious Deaths Around the Tees, Maureen Anderson
ISBN: 1-903425-26-3   £9.99

More Foul Deeds and Suspicious Deaths in Wakefield, Kate Taylor
ISBN: 1-903425-48-4   £9.99

Foul Deeds and Suspicious Deaths in York, Keith Henson
ISBN: 1-903425-33-6   £9.99

Foul Deeds and Suspicious Deaths on the Yorkshire Coast, Alan Whitworth
ISBN: 1-903425-01-8   £9.99

Foul Deeds and Suspicious Deaths in Coventry, David McGrory
ISBN: 1-903425-57-3   £9.99

Foul Deeds and Suspicious Deaths in Manchester, Martin Baggoley
ISBN: 1-903425-65-4   £9.99

Foul Deeds and Suspicious Deaths in and Around Newcastle,
Maureen Anderson
ISBN: 1-903425-34-4   £9.99

Foul Deeds and Suspicious Deaths Around Oxfordshire, Carl Boardman
ISBN: 1-903425-56-5   £9.99

Foul Deeds and Suspicious Deaths Around Pontefract and Castleford, Keith Henson
ISBN: 1-903425-54-9   £9.99

Please contact us via any of the methods below for more information or a catalogue.
WHARNCLIFFE BOOKS
47 Church Street – Barnsley – South Yorkshire – S70 2AS
Tel: 01226 734555 – 734222 Fax: 01226 724438
E-mail: enquiries@pen-and-sword.co.uk - Website: www.wharncliffebooks.co.uk

Foul Deeds & Suspicious Deaths Around
NEWPORT

TERRY UNDERWOOD

Series Editor
Brian Elliott

Wharncliffe Books

First published in Great Britain in 2005 by
Wharncliffe Books
An imprint of
Pen & Sword Books Ltd
47 Church Street
Barnsley
South Yorkshire
S70 2AS

Copyright © Terry Underwood, 2005

ISBN 1-903425-59-X

Typeset in 11/13pt Plantin by Andy Hemingway, Barnsley.

Printed and bound in England
By CPI UK

Pen & Sword Books Ltd incorporates the Imprints of
Pen & Sword Aviation, Pen & Sword Maritime,
Pen & Sword Military, Wharncliffe Books,
Pen & Sword Select, Pen & Sword Military Classics
and Leo Cooper.

For a complete list of Pen & Sword titles please contact
PEN & SWORD BOOKS LIMITED
47 Church Street,
Barnsley,
South Yorkshire,
S70 2AS,
England
E-mail: enquiries@pen-and-sword.co.uk
Website: www.pen-and-sword.co.uk

Contents

Acknowledgements

The author would like to thank the following parties for their assistance in the production of this book:

The *South Wales Argus* for their permission to publish excerpts from their admirable local newspaper, especially the editor, Gerry Keighley and his staff.

The staff of Abertillery Library and the staff of Newport Reference Library who offered continuous assistance and advice during the five months of research for the book, also merit my appreciation.

A special thank you to Kenneth Smith and Ann Bailey who both provided leads.

To Leslie Davies, Terry O'Neil, David Husband, Chief Superintendent Kevin Price and retired Chief Inspector Billie Glynn for their valuable information.

To Rex Morton, Peter Brown and Mr WG Lloyd, who supplied photographs, and to Tom Tasker for his technical support.

Thanks are also due to Tony Friend and (for photographs of the Odeon Cinema, Bristol, and its manager) Chris Plaister.

I would also like to thank the publishers, Wharncliffe Books who requested I write this book and Rupert Harding and Brian Elliott for their encouragement.

My love and thanks to my wife Hazel for supporting me in all my efforts and to my daughter Debbie for her contribution.

Introduction

The Killing Fields
AD 74

[When] *death was a sport and life was cheap, the taking of it meaningless.*

When someone dear to you dies, there is a never-ending grief for those who are left behind. They say that time heals, but in reality, one simply becomes used to their absence. If, however, a loved one is murdered, there is always the feeling of having been robbed of their company. No matter how much time passes, the injustice remains an added burden to the grieving. Often, the sheer horror of their death haunts and repulses the family forever. Worse than this is the knowledge that one member of the family took the life of another relative, then, there is a double loss. To continue to live with the memory and avoid the stain that permeates the rest of your days must be one of the most difficult achievements. Families are broken, communities are ruptured and locations bear, for eternity, the shadow of evil that once occurred in that place.

The rest of us, who have never had to experience such treachery, remain distressed, disturbed and curious as to the nature of the murderer, particularly as we can sometimes comprehend, for example a crime of passion, or loss of self-control. Other murders are far more sinister and unfathomable, madness or perversion, that leads to the taking of someone's life, will always remain beyond understanding. We will continue to wonder at the twisted mentality of Jack the Ripper, in whose mind society was being 'cleaned up.' The fact that his sin was greater than the sin of the prostitutes he killed was not a consideration. If we take Fred and Rosemary West as an example, one is aware that their deeds began with small perversions, and in the effort to satiate their growing desire for more and more extreme gratification, each person who entered their world were subjected to their abuses. Eventually, murder takes place merely to silence a witness.

Some victims are the product of one manic moment, and others from the development of mental illness. The brutality that a soldier is forced to endure for the sake of his country is barbaric, this acceptance and justification for the taking of another's life, can lead to a moral decline towards butchery and the devaluation of life. The interest in murder will remain a subject to occasionally ponder, whether it's the taking of life in a war, or for the purpose of justice, or to relieve someone of their suffering. 'Thou shalt not kill' is a fundamental part of the nobility of man, and it is right that we should understand and define the boundaries in each case.

From the beginning of history, justice has sought to maintain law and order. Those who are Christians will know that the first recorded murder in the Bible was that of Cain killing his brother Abel. God's response to this was to curse Cain with a long life, that he might endure the suffering of his sin until his final judgement. That 'vengeance is mine,' sayeth the Lord, is a theme continued in the New Testament when Jesus asks that 'who among you is without sin shall cast the first stone,' the adulterous woman was told to go and sin no more. Once again we see the continuation of life for the sinner and the right of society to be relieved of the burden to take revenge. The subject of capital punishment is as complicated and as old as mankind itself. Whether it is better to seek revenge and justice, to save money for the taxpayer, and to serve as a warning to the rest of us is still debateable.

The Roman amphitheatre, in particular the Colisseum, was an original forum of justice. Criminals were forced to become gladiators who, by their bravery in the arena, could redeem themselves. Many a perpetrator of crime became a popular, thumbs down, hero by displaying his fearlessness. The popularity of each emperor rested upon his provision of entertainment for the public, and the crowds that encircled the ring became more and more addicted to re-enactments of valour and the pursuit of justice. The mob was swept along in the bloodthirsty circus of death.

Due to low-lying, waterlogged land that was impossible to build upon, the city of Newport was formerly known as

Pendan. It was here that the Romans tried to settle in AD74. It was decided that the near-by area of Caerleon was more suitable, so the 2nd legion from Rome re-named the place *Isca* and set up camp. Pendan was in decline whilst the Roman fortress in *Isca* became more and more popular. *Isca* drew the masses from other towns and gradually its population swelled into a hive of trade and activity over the further 200 years of Roman occupation.

The Romans had brought an army of 5,000 men and an additional 1,000 civilians who were primarily trades people. The building of the fortress included six areas of barrack accommodation, a hospital fortress, baths, workshops and an army headquarters. Around the forty-eight acres, a high defensive wall was built and outside the walls they built additional baths and a magnificent amphitheatre and parade ground. Much of this remains today and is still a place of public interest in Newport.

All large events were staged at the amphitheatre, which could hold up to 6,000 people. Here, gladiators were forced to provide entertainment for the massive population by fighting

A re-enactment of gladiators fighting to the death in Caerleon Roman ampitheatre in c. AD74. The Killing Fields can be seen in the far background.

The Roman ampitheatre at Caerleon, built in AD74, which could hold up to 6000 people. Gladiators were forced to provide entertainment for the massive population by fighting to the death.

to the death. Rebel slaves were often put to death by crucifixion. Chariot racing was a favourite Roman pastime and if a member of the public got in the way it was hard luck. Famous gladiators became celebrities that glittered in the centre of the cheering crowds. When someone was slaughtered in the arena, the sound of the cheering mob would have travelled up as far as Christchurch Hill. The thrill of the crowd was infectious and raucous, much like today when a goal is scored, those outside the stadium can hear the roar of success or the massive groan of failure, death was a sport and life was cheap, the taking of it, meaningless.

Near Christchurch, in an area known as St Julian's Wood, the Roman citizens and local people would take those whom they wished to dispose of. It was in this area that innocent victims were slaughtered and left to rot. The quiet fields and secluded woods became known in those times as the Killing Fields. The bodies of those who had offended or who had been unable to pay their debts lay here unburied. It was an ideal place to take the law into your own hands, quiet enough for rape, close enough for the rapid removal of an enemy. No one interfered when the screams floated across the river; no one with any sense took a walk in that place and no one investigated the goings on after an event.

Even in a society where death was the appropriate punishment for crime, where death was part of everyday life, where death was entertainment, there was still a section of society that sought to murder in secret.

The following stories from Newport and its surrounding villages are a warning to the innocent to avoid danger, a tribute to those who solved the crimes, a recognition for the bereaved, a remembrance to those who died and a testimony to the beast within.

A view of the St Julian's Woods taken from Christchurch and used by the Romans as the Killing Fields.

CHAPTER 1

Till Death Us Do Part
1650s

*A few minutes later Edmund was dead, his white shirt was red, the
sword having penetrated his heart.*

Caerleon, a small village that was once the Roman city
of Isca, is now an expanded and vital part of
Newport. History tells us that in AD75, Isca was the
only Roman Fortress sited on the banks of the River Usk. It
had a shipping port long before Newport and the Roman
archaeology remains visible even today. The foundations of the
large Roman Barracks are still there, together with the remains
of Roman Baths and an Amphitheatre, which is still used. In
the summer season, Roman displays and re-enactments are
held at the Amphitheatre. Caerleon also lays claim to being the
location of Camelot, where King Arthur and his Knights of the
Round Table originated.

In the early 1600s, Thomas Williams, a wealthy land and ship
owner, lived in Caerleon with his wife. In 1633 Thomas and his
wife had a son whom they christened Charles. By the time
Charles was fifteen years old he was well known, likeable, and
happy, being the only son of a prosperous father, he was also
considered to be a good prospect for marriage.

Charles had a cousin called Edmund Morgan; Edmund also
lived in Caerleon and was equally as popular as Charles.
Throughout their teenage years, one was rarely seen without
the other, as cousins they were the best of friends. They had
two close companions, John Hanbury and Robert Cox. When
the four boys went out and about in the village they always
attracted attention, playing games together on the Common,
fishing in the local rivers or dancing in the inns; in general, they
were much involved with the community, and everywhere they
went they were the life and soul of the party.

Robert Cox, a bright young man of twenty-four, had a sister
named Annabelle. She was eighteen years old, very sweet, with

an outgoing personality. When she first met her brother's three friends, it was Charles Williams who first caught her eye, and soon gained her full attention. Everyone noticed that Charles was besotted with Annabelle, and Charles occasionally took time away from his 'Gang of Four' in order to be with Annabelle.

The romance between Charles and Annabelle flourished, it was a serious relationship and everyone in Caerleon knew this. Many of the villagers were looking forward to the day when they would marry. When, like a bolt from the sky, Charles discovered that his cousin Edmund was also seeing Annabelle on occasions, Charles was seen to be hurt and outraged. How deep the involvement between Annabelle and Edmund was not known, but Charles was so angered by the development that the four friends became estranged. The lifelong harmony between Charles and Edmund no longer existed, snide remarks were being made which infuriated Charles even further, and in a moment of rage, Charles challenged his cousin Edmund to a duel.

In the 1650s, sword fencing to the death was no longer legal, and for one human to kill another amounted to murder. Edmund and Charles were quite accustomed to fencing, but only used swords with a small metal guard on the tip of the blade. Whether Edmund thought that this was the arrangement for the duel was not known, but Edmund agreed to the contest, and the time and the place were decided upon.

John Hanbury and Robert Cox talked to Charles about this, and tried to talk him out of the duel, but Charles was adamant that the duel should take place as planned, and so he invited them to accompany him.

A quiet place had been chosen between Afon Lwyd and Candwr Brook, a small island further on up the Usk River. There, the four former best friends gathered in a state of nervousness, not knowing what the outcome would be. Before the duel commenced, they shook hands then immediately pulled swords. The fight began. For the first minute or so the duel seemed equal, as both men danced around each other in the brilliant sunshine. Their swords clashed, they gasped for breath, occasionally shouting to their opponent, Hanbury and

St Cadoc's church, Caerleon, where Charles Williams first hid after killing Edmund Cox in 1660.

Cox standing in silence, demonstrating their neutrality. They wished that the fight had never started. Suddenly with a loud cry Charles Williams lunged forward and Edmund fell to his knees with a look of astonishment on his face. Blood was pouring from his chest. Almost immediately, Charles rushed forward shouting 'No Edmund, No!' He knelt to hold Edmund and cried, 'Please Edmund, don't die.' Charles was in tears; the sound of his voice filled the air and sent a flock of birds screeching into the sky. For a moment, the two spectators stood in disbelief, and then suddenly rushed forward to comfort Charles and Edmund. A few minutes later Edmund was dead, his white shirt was red, the sword having penetrated his heart. Charles was never known to cry, but here he was reduced to tears, saying over and over again, 'Edmund, I'm sorry, I'm sorry, please forgive me.'

Unbeknown to them, the farmer who owned the land on

The Handbury Arms *in Caerleon, now part of Newport, where in 1660 Charles Williams hid after killing Edmund Cox. The second place of hiding.*

The top of the Blackash Path where Annabelle Cox would take a basket of food and drink for Charles Williams.

which the duel had taken place had been watching the event from a short distance, behind some trees. He came forward and offered a horse and cart so that Edmund's body could be taken back to Caerleon. As the cortege made its way through the streets of Caerleon, crowds gathered and stood in horrified silence, not knowing what had happened. By the time the cart had reached St Cadoc's church in the High Street, the story was out and Charles was jeered as he walked behind the body and entered the church.

The local authorities saw this as an act of murder and immediately sent out the watchmen of the day to arrest Charles but by the time they arrived at St Cadoc's Church, Charles was nowhere to be found. It was said that Charles had hidden at the back of the church, and then, with the help of John Hanbury, under the cover of darkness, had moved across the road to the *Hanbury Inn*. The *Hanbury Arms*, as it is now known, still stands on the bank of the River Usk, next to Caerleon Bridge.

Annabelle Cox, now full of remorse, was told by John Hanbury, that Charles was hiding there and that he would welcome a visit from her. The meeting was arranged and a few more followed. Between the couple, all was forgiven but danger came close when the watchmen made a thorough search of the inn, but found nothing.

Charles realised he would have to make another move, this time he went over the wooden bridge that spanned the Usk, along the road that led to a narrow pathway which led to the top of the hill to Christchurch. The lane is called The Black Ash Path. Charles hid himself in Christchurch church where Annabelle delivered baskets of food to him. She was seen on a few occasions with the basket, walking up the Black Ash Path. Realising that people would get suspicious, Annabelle told Charles he would have to leave Christchurch and return to the *Hanbury Inn*. At high tide, one of his father's ships would be leaving for Turkey, and Charles had been invited to join it. On the quayside at the rear of the Hanbury, in the still of night, Charles said his goodbyes to Annabelle; he promised that one day he would return.

Charles Williams sailed to Turkey and settled in Smyrna, where, he became a rich fig merchant. In 1690 Charles wrote a letter which enquired about the schools in Caerleon. Now a very wealthy man and living in London, he lived and moved in high society, and upon hearing that Caerleon was a very poor place with no school, he decided to do something about it. At about this time Charles had become a personal friend of Sarah,

The start of Blackash Path in Caerleon that Annabelle Cox travelled up daily to take food to Christchurch church for Charles Williams.

Duchess of Marlborough who was the most influential person at the court of Queen Anne. It was through their friendship that Queen Anne was persuaded to grant a 'Pardon' to Charles Williams. After making more enquiries at Caerleon, Charles made a loan to the Bank of England for the sum of £3,000, this was done in 1694, and in 1715 large amounts of money were set aside for the building of the Williams Charity School in Caerleon. Thus the Blue Coat school of Caerleon was born.

Charles died in October 1720 and had never returned to Caerleon, although in his will he expressed a wish to be buried in his native town; however, his friends thought otherwise, and he was buried under the north aisle in Westminster Abbey where his memorial can still be seen today.

Christchurch Church at the top of Blackash Path where Charles Williams hid after killing Edmund Cox in 1660, the third place of hiding.

CHAPTER 2

Mass Murder in Westgate Square
1839

... they [the soldiers] *shot randomly into the crowd and innocent men lost their lives.*

On the fourth day of November 1839, an army of discontented civilian men marched down to Newport from the surrounding valleys. The rebels, now known as the Chartist Rioters, numbered well over 8,000 and were mainly unarmed, apart from the picks and pikes they were carrying.

They were involved in an uprising that left twenty-two bodies lying dead on the cobblestone streets of Newport. The incident occurred mainly in the Westgate Square of the town and the lower end of Stow Hill. Many more died on their way home from the encounter, or later at their homes from wounds they received at the Westgate from British soldiers. Two Officers and their men were waiting in the *Westgate Hotel*, in the centre of Newport. The troops were using the hotel as a fortress.

A Swansea newspaper published at the time said that the final number killed could reach sixty. Many died quietly at

The Westgate Hotel in Westgate Square, Newport, where twenty-two people died. At least forty others died from their wounds after they had left the scene of the attack, 4 November 1839

their homes in secret, due to the shame that their families were experiencing and the consequent disgrace of having been related to a rebel. Those who died on their way home were buried in fields or woodland glades, miles from where they actually lived. Neighbours were informed that those who died weeks or months after their injuries, had in fact, died of natural causes. The cover-up was necessary to avoid any connection with the Westgate Massacre and so that the families could go on living without a blemish on the family name.

These men had gathered together to protest against their working conditions. The majority of them were unarmed, hungry and appalled at having to work with children as young as five years of age. It was not unusual for there to be disturbances in the valleys, the poverty and deprivation inflicted on whole communities by the owners of the mines was beyond the pale. To make matters worse, many of the pits were closed completely, leaving the men that had families to support totally unemployed.

Those that were still employed were paid mostly with company tokens. These tokens could only be used in the company shops which meant that the profits went straight back into the pockets of the company. Often the company shop sold inferior goods or gave small portions: sometimes workers would mortgage their wages in advance so that they could feed their families.

The suffering and repression caused widespread discontent. Everyone wanted something to be done, but the ironmasters would not listen, in fact they formed their own organisation to protect their own interests. The workers would discuss their plight in public houses or with their neighbours in each other's homes. Eventually these pockets of resistance developed into secret societies and lodges.

Because of the lack of sensitivity towards the workers and the personal greed of the owners, these small societies developed into sinister unions that would become as terrifying in their demands as the owners were with their limitations. The union ringleaders were known as Scotch Cattle, since in order to avoid being recognised they blackened their faces and wore the skins of animals. The rules were simple and reasonable but they were enforced in a brutal and intimidating manner. It was agreed that there should be a limit on the amount of labour available, that only the children of employed men should apply for work and that those seeking employment should contribute into the Lodge fund. Anyone breaking these rules might find their homes vandalised or worse, be grievously harmed. The employers were systematically destroying the community by keeping them exhausted and impoverished and the new union leaders were bullies. It was in this awful situation that the scene was set for the Chartist Riots.

The reformers had Chartist songs, newspapers and a few prominent orators. One of these orators distinguished himself on the podium and became the leader of reform. His name was John Frost. John was a Newport born businessman and former Mayor of the town: he was well liked, very eloquent and encouraging. In Nantyglo another good speaker rose to lead the people, his name Zephania Williams and in Pontypool there was a William Jones. Both of these men became Lieutenants to the Chartist leader, Frost.

In March 1839 Henry Vincent was arrested at Monmouth for inciting people to riot. Henry was a member of the London Workingmen's Association and one of its finest orators. At only twenty-five he was already well travelled and had a great fervour for political reform. John Frost often gave speeches at the same events as Henry. They knew each other, and had the same aim, which was that employees should be protected from inhumane treatment.

Henry's arrest was the spark that lit the fuse, the freedom to discuss their working and living conditions had failed, no-one had listened to their discontent, no-one cared how many hours they had to work for a pittance, they could starve for all it mattered. Something would have to done.

The Lord Lieutenant of the County and the Secretary of State became aware that there would be civil unrest and they took part in anti-Chartist meetings. The people of Newport heard that there was to be a protest march into the town and many of them stayed away from work in case there was trouble. A detachment of soldiers moved into Newport, 120 or more strong, and London policemen were sent down to organise the

The Chartist riot at the Westgate Hotel, *Newport.*

special constables who had enrolled in Newport. The Mayor, Thomas Phillips, asked the people to remain calm and he also ordered that the troops be transferred to the central postion of the *Westgate Hotel.* The shutters of the hotel were closed so that the soldiers presence could not be misconstrued as a challenge to the protesters.

On Friday, 1 November 1839, Frost held his final meeting at the *Coach and Horses Inn,* Blackwood. Zephania Williams and William Jones planned to meet with their men at the Cefn, Rogerstone. The plan was to destroy Newport's only bridge (thus preventing the mail getting through to London) and then to march on to Monmouth to secure the release of Henry Vincent from gaol.

On Monday, 4 November, 8,000 men mustered together and began their march to Newport. Lightly armed with farm implements, a few had guns, and many sang Chartist songs under the influence of drink. By the time they reached the Welsh Oak, great numbers of the men were too drunk to take any orders. Frost decided to wait for a while in order for the men to sober up, this would also give Jones and his men time to join up with the marchers at Cefn.

Whilst at the Cefn, Frost instructed two of his men, under the cover of darkness, to go into Newport to assess the situation. There were troops stationed at the top of Stow Hill, who discovered the two men upon their mission. These were taken as hostages to the *Westgate Hotel.* Word was sent back to

The Newport Chartist riot continues.

the Chartists that they were being held prisoner with the troops based at the hotel. Before they could continue with their plans to advance their cause by blowing up the bridge, they now had to secure the release of their two fellow reformers.

Finally, they arrived in Newport and John Frost gave the order 'To the Westgate' in order to release the men from their captors. When they arrived they were horrified to find that the troops were waiting in ambush at the Westgate. As the massive crowd streamed down Stow Hill, the townspeople fled in all directions from them as they swarmed into Westgate Square.

Frost stood at the head of his men and those with firearms pointed towards the hotel. Suddenly, from an upstairs window, the Mayor, Thomas Phillips, appeared. For a moment there was silence, then the mob began to shout 'Reform' and Frost was lost in the tidal wave of revolt that followed.

It has been said that the first shot was fired accidentally, and no one knew from which side it came, but within seconds the fighting and shooting was rife, Westgate Square was filled with smoke. The Mayor shouted from the window 'Lay down your arms.' A second later the Mayor reeled back into the arms of Lieutenant Grey. He had been shot in the arm and groin. At this, the soldiers moved to the front windows and opened fire. They shot randomly into the crowd and innocent men lost their lives. The majority of the Chartists were making a peaceful protest and when they saw the havoc that was breaking out in their front ranks, many of them began to disperse.

Later that night John Frost was arrested at a friend's house. The police used force to gain entry and the Police Superintendent shouted out 'We represent the law', to which Frost replied, 'The law demands so much. To break it is to adjust a changing world. The people demand adjustment in their time.' 'Hold your fire' cried the Superintendent. Then Frost said, 'Let the tongue replace the pistol. No more bloodshed.' And with that Frost was led quietly away.

Frost, Williams and Jones were found guilty of High Treason, with a recommendation for mercy. Henry Vincent carried on the fight for the lives of the three leaders from an adjacent cell. Early in February 1840 the prisoners were taken to Chepstow where they boarded the steamer *Usk* bound for Portsmouth from which they eventually sailed to Australia on the convict ship *Mandarin*. Frost, at the age of fifty-four was to spend the next fourteen years away from these shores and his family.

This was the final scene of one of the greatest political tragedies in British history. In March 1854 the three men were pardoned, but only Frost returned to this country. On his first visit to Newport after his transportation, he received a tremendous welcome when he was drawn through the town in a flower-decked open carriage. Crowds lined the streets and brought tears to his eyes once more as he left the carriage to re-enter the same hotel that has given Newport – sad as it may be – a permanent place in history – The Westgate.

These are the names of those who were massacred, despite their own personal innocence: they lost their lives for a cause that we can all understand. We remember them along with all those in the world who have had to resort to protest in order for the rest of us to have employment law and civil rights:

John Codd, David Davies, David Davies (son), Evan Davies, John David, William Evans, William Farraday, John Jonathan, William Griffiths, Robert Lansdown, Reece Meredith, David Morgan, John Morris, George Shell, Abraham Thomas, Isaac Thomas, Ben Williams, William Williams, William Aberdare, John The Roller, Harold Cox and Bertie Hall.

They were shot in the genuine pursuit of justice.

CHAPTER 3

The Mudcrawlers
1840s

These are the remains of our Irish cousins who drowned in the mud, unable to take refuge from us without endangering their lives.

Murder, however it is committed, is always unacceptable, unjustified and usually sickening. The motives for murder do vary; sometimes we can understand why the act is committed, whilst other murders are totally unfathomable. It has consequences beyond the loss of life. There can be the destruction of a family, grief for friends, horror for those that investigate and terror for those who live nearby. Furthermore, a location becomes tainted and society as a whole is degenerated to savagery. When whole families go missing, never to be seen or heard of again, it is then that the community suffers the most.

There were many cases of this nature that occurred in Newport and its surrounding districts in the early eighteen hundreds. During this period, the Newport coastline was awash with mud, slush and murky water. When the Romans came to Britain in AD75, they arrived from the Bristol Channel, and then entered the River Usk. They did not stay in the area because tidal waters from the Bristol Channel frequently covered the ground, especially at Spring tide. The Romans would continue upstream for about three miles before disembarking from their vessels and settling down on the dry land that became known as *Isca*, now Caerleon.

At high tide, most of Newport's lowland became waterlogged. Parts of an area called Pillgwenlly became small islands with tidal water only receding once it had reached the now main Cardiff Road. The Royal Gwent Hospital is now located here. In the 1700s the only bridge that Newport had was constructed from timber with loose planks of wood across the road section. When high tides arrived, which were at times as high as forty-eight feet, the planks of wood were allowed to float around until the tide receded, then they were replaced, but not nailed down. If someone wanted to travel to London from Newport, they could not use the Chepstow Road or Maindee Square because of the flooding. The traveller would be obliged to make their way up Church Road to Christchurch Road, Newport's highest point, then along Catsash Road until they reached dry ground.

In the early 1800s, Newport was a port without proper docking facilities, all shipping would moor against the banks of the River Usk, mainly on the west side from Newport Castle, down to the mouth of the river and Bristol Channel. By 1820, Newport began to thrive, and coal was being shipped by barge, down to Newport's riverbank for loading upon ships. Newport was exporting many other goods as well as coal. Business was booming and Newport was expanding rapidly. It was not the same story for a small harbour in North Devon, called Appledore. Situated on the north coast of Devon, Appledore was economically depressed and many ships were no longer active. One such ship, the *Sarah Maria Anne*, was owned by John Fisher who also captained the ship. Before the depression, he had employed about six of the local men as crew. Captain John Fisher was desperate for work and had heard about the ongoing prosperity and hive of activity in Newport, so he decided to cross over the Bristol Channel and establish his shipping business there.

Part of the mouth of the Bristol Channel at the mouth of the river Usk and used by the Mudcrawlers in the 1840s.

The *Sarah Maria Anne* soon became part of the Newport shipping and export scene, by shipping merchandise and livestock to Cork in southern Ireland. The primary cargo was coal. Cork was the main port and the activity between Newport and Cork increased daily. On the return journeys Irish potatoes were brought back but, after a few months in operation, Captain Fisher discovered another commodity that was being shipped to Newport, and that commodity was human.

In 1820, poverty had hit Ireland so hard that a large proportion of its population began to look for an improved quality of life. The Branigans, the Flanigans, the Doughertys, and the Donovans were all searching for a better life: they thought that it might be found in Britain. In 1825 Newport belonged to Monmouthshire, which when referred to was, 'Not in England, and not in Wales.' Newport became a target for the then desperate Irish families. The O'Briens, O'Harras, O'Gradys and the O'Marras were all determined to leave their homeland, and many of them could be seen queuing at the quayside of Cork harbour, hoping for a space on any British ship that would take them to a new life. For around £3 per head, some Irish families thought that they were going as far as America, but it was Newport they were heading for. Families of two, three, four and more would arrive at Cork harbour carrying bundles of clothes and other valuable goods to help them once they arrived in this country. Captain John Fisher was one of the seamen prepared to transport these people, and once at Newport they would leave the ship and make their way inland to an unknown destination.

Newport did employ three or four watchmen to oversee operations on the riverbank, and they were aware that large numbers of Irish families were leaving the moored ships to settle in Newport. The authorities in Newport decided that far too many people were coming into the town and made a local law, which made it illegal to enter the country in this manner. The watchmen were given the task of putting this new law into effect. From then on, the Irish families were ordered to re-embark upon the ship, and the captains were told to take them back to Ireland. Ship owners were reluctant to do this, having carried them this far; they had, by then, become acquainted with them and had taken care of them on the journey. They were to be pitied, as there was no work and no food in Ireland and somehow they had to survive, but the watchmen would not permit their entry.

The skippers of a large number of a large number of vessels got together and decided to take them back to Cork. Alternatively, they could travel back as far as the mouth of the River Usk to an area called St Brides, where they could jump overboard. They would have to trail through muddy water, then, on their hands and knees they could make their way to the land by crawling through the mud on the embankments. Hundreds of Irish families decided to do this rather than return to poverty and deprivation. In the mud, many of them lost their few remaining possessions or the last of the food they had brought with them.

From that point on they were known as the 'Mudcrawlers.' Once ashore they would either walk back to Newport, which risked deportation or walk to an area known as Peterstone, which was less hazardous. Others went on into mid-Wales, and some further north. The Mudcrawlers now formed a large part of the Pilgwenlly community. They settled well into the friendly town of Newport and did indeed enjoy much better prospects than they had endured in Ireland.

Not every story had a happy ending and some families disappeared, never to be seen again, whilst they were homeless, they became easy targets for thieves, rapists and murderers. Of course some families needed to become obscure, but others had hoped to integrate with the community and not to become victims of the community. Sometimes, when relatives came over to Wales from Ireland, hoping to trace their families or friends, they returned home very disappointed and sometimes greatly disturbed.

Since 1840 a large number of buildings have been developed. When digging the foundations, builders have frequently reported the finding of human bones. These are the remains of our Irish cousins who drowned in the mud, unable to take refuge amongst us without endangering their lives. Without an identity they would not be missed and without homes, all their worldly good were on their backs, easy pickings! In some locations, nearer to the banks of the river there lie the remains of the children that couldn't make it to shore. There in the dark, trying to be quiet, terrified of being discovered and sent home to starve, parents would hiss their children's names, every moment expecting them to appear. They had been wading through the mud together, everyone struggling along, almost there, then suddenly the weakest would be swept away or sucked down into the mud. To risk starvation or drowning? The adults who walked away would never be able to answer that.

In 1849 two Irishmen left southern Ireland, by boarding the *Sarah Maria Ann* cargo ship. It was due to sail back home to Newport, their names were Sullivan and Murphy. They arrived at Newport after having a rough crossing, and were more than happy to set foot on the banks of the River Usk. They had very little money and were desperate to find lodgings and perhaps some supper. They noticed a stream of people walking down, what today is known as Lower Dock Street, and you know the old saying 'where there's muck there's money' so Sullivan and Murphy joined the trail. They had no idea where they were going, all that mattered was that somehow, amongst these people they would be able to obtain money. Eventually they arrived at Newport cattle market, the ideal place to rip someone off. Along with hundreds of other people they jostled about, some were buying, some were selling – but both had cash.

The criminal annals of the county record a most atrocious murder in the year 1849, when a Mrs Lewis, an aged woman, living at Nantcoch farm, was murdered. At the market, she had just sold a cow for a good price. It was when Sullivan and Murphy saw the transaction that they decided she would provide them with the money they needed. The unfortunate woman was attacked in the highway as she was returning from Newport market. She was killed outright, and her body was dragged into a hedge, which bounded the turnpike road. It was not, however the woman who had sold the cow. The intended victim was a Mrs Edwards of Cefn Parva farm; it was Mrs Edwards who had made a tidy sum when selling the cow. The woman in the hedge had nothing on her.

Frustrated at their lack of success, Sullivan and Murphy fled to Cheltenham empty-handed. Another opportunity presented itself on the way. A farmer was their next victim, brutally attacked and left for dead, but this time Murphy and Sullivan had not only money but also a watch. They were apprehended at Cheltenham, tried shortly afterwards, and sentenced to death. Neither repented of their actions, and both died declaring their innocence.

The lighthouse at St Brides, near the mouth of the River Usk, used by the Mudcrawlers in the 1840s.

CHAPTER 4

Caught in Time
1874

The police opened the watch and read the inscription, it was all they needed to know: they had a prime suspect.

James Henry Gibbs was a tall handsome man, elegant, graceful and refined to say the least, and a very popular man, especially where ladies were concerned. Gibbs, who was married to Susan, a lady much older than her husband, lived for most of the time alone in Cardiff, due to the nature of James's job. He was employed by a Mr Williams of Llanrumny Hall as a butler to the stately home at St Mellon's, between Newport and Cardiff. Gibbs, who always played the part as the head butler, and always looked the part, wore a watch on a chain, a gift from his wife Susan. The watch was sparkling silver, engraved with the words 'to my loving husband, James, from your wife, Susan'. The watch was always more outside of his waistcoat pocket than in, as he was always ready to deliver the time to anyone that requested it.

James was a ladies' man and he had formed an acquaintance with a much younger lady than his wife. James requested a meeting with Susan to discuss a separation on 12 May 1874. At that meeting, they took a walk to a nearby farm that was owned by Samuel West, a local farmer. Later the same evening James returned to Llanrumney Hall to continue with his duties as head butler. Some weeks later, Susan Ann Gibbs, wife of James Henry Gibbs was reported missing. A search was made by police in the area of Cardiff and of St Mellons, however there was no result. Gibbs continued to play the part of the perfect butler, occasionally approaching the police to request news from his wife Susan. But nothing came, and life went on, and the case of the missing person faded in time.

Some time later, farmer Samuel West and his eight-year-old granddaughter, took a walk across the fields of the farm. A bright glint in the grass caught Rachel's eye, and she stooped to take a look. 'Grandad, look, I've found a watch.' The chain was stuck in the mud, so Rachel pulled, and the chain was attached to a decaying hand. The police were informed, and at the scene of the crime, close investigations began. Rachel stood aside and touched nothing, as her grandfather had asked her to do. The police opened the watch and read the inscription, it was all they needed to know: they had a prime suspect. Meanwhile, Gibbs the butler, continued to supply the time to anyone who requested it. He used a similar watch to the one that Susan held in her hand.

The plan was for a small number of police officers to lay wait to see if Gibbs would visit the scene of the crime, to recover his

William Marwood (1874-1883), the public executioner, who pioneered the 'long-drop', a more humane, or at least quicker death for the condemned murderer.
Brian Elliott Collection

engraved watch. It was 3 June 1874, when the body of Susan Ann Gibbs was discovered in a shallow grave on Llanrumney farm, by then she was decomposing. On a nightime watch, the figure of a man was seen entering the field: he walked towards the scene of the crime. It was him, Gibbs. The police watched as he stood over the grave. The moon supplied enough light for Gibbs to see at once the skeletal hand that clasped his watch. The police rushed forward and arrested James Henry Gibbs. He broke free, they chased, and two fields later, they had their man.

Gibbs went on trial on 6 August 1874, within two days, he was found guilty of murder. The court, at Monmouth Assizes, sentenced him to death. He was executed at Usk Prison, on Monday, 24 August, by the hangman, Marwood. He never confessed his guilt.

At the gallows, Gibbs was dragged, kicking and screaming to his end, the scene was shocking. He called upon The Almighty to testify to his innocence, crying out, 'God forgive me for all my past sins.' 'He knows that I am innocent, and I am happy that he knows I am innocent, I die innocent.' Gibbs stood on the gallows, shackled and shaking, 'Goodbye my parents, goodbye all, may The Almighty have mercy upon me.' Marwood placed the rope around his neck, and time ran out for James Henry Gibbs.

The execution of Gibbs was the first to have taken place in Usk since the closure of the County Gaol at Monmouth.

CHAPTER 5

Bloody Murder at Llangibby
1878

A tearful sight met his gaze when he reached the gate...

In a small picturesque village just five miles outside Newport, it's very difficult to imagine an horrific event that occurred in 1878. Not only did the crime shock Llangibby to the core, but Newport also felt the impact, as did the whole nation of Great Britain.

The crime took place on 17 July 1878; so dreadful was the killing of five members of one family that the *Monmouthshire Merlin*, a local newspaper at the time, described the tragedy as 'unparalleled in atrocity in the annals of crime of Great Britain'.

To visit the village one should pass through Caerleon, on the outskirts of Newport and head towards Usk for about five miles. You will arrive at one of Gwent's quieter and rustic villages, Llangibby.

On Thursday, 18 July 1878, at around 6.30 am, a young boy named Frank James was seen making his way up a sloping

The centre of this photograph is where the cottage of the Watkins family once stood.

A rare photograph showing the cottage at Llangibby, where the Watkins family was murdered in July 1878.

path, through an early morning mist, to a small cottage. A farm labourer called William Watkins, his wife Eliza, and their three children, Charlotte (aged 8), Frederick (5) and Alice (4), occupied the cottage.

Young Frank James had been hoeing swede with William Watkins the previous day at Cwm Farm. The boy went to the cottage to call Mr Watkins, for it was noticed at the farm near by that he was unusually late that morning. A fearful sight met his gaze when he reached the gate of the small garden and path leading up to the cottage door.

Happily for the little boy, he did not grasp the fearfulness of the scene, he turned and ran back to the village and told his mother that a man was asleep in the garden. The impression that something was wrong seems to have been gathered from the scared expression on the lad's face. The mother and son went to the *White Hart Inn* and woke up the landlord, Ernest George. He contacted a Mr Day who lived nearby. Together with several others they sped to the cottage. What they saw would have remained in their memories for the rest of their lives.

Mr George gave the following statement to a reporter:

It was this morning, about seven o'clock, when the little boy and his mother came to the White Hart Inn and said 'Mrs Watkins is killed.' I went up to the cottage at once to see what was the matter, the spot being not more than half a mile from here (the White Hart Inn). When I got there I found Mrs Watkins lying inside the gate; her husband was lying dead about four yards from her, smoke was then issuing from the top of the house, and a number of people soon collected. The door leading into the cottage was not fastened, I went in with Mr Day, and we found that the door leading to the upstairs bedroom was closed. We succeeded in opening this door but the stench from what smelt like burning sulphur, was so powerful that we could not go in. So we went outside, and broke some slates on the roof. This let some of the stench out, and with Mr Day we went back into the cottage and into the bedroom. There was blood everywhere. One child was lying under one bed, and there were two lying upon another bed. There were three beds in the room; the eldest child was about eight years old. We placed them all carefully on the boards. They were quite dead. We threw some water on the bed, which was smouldering, and after that, leaving the children there, we returned downstairs and into the garden. One of the eldest child's legs was put up as though crossed over the other leg; it was burnt black. The leg of the other child was clean burnt off above the ankle, and the third one too was very much burnt. The beds were almost entirely destroyed. The downstairs was in great confusion. Books, papers and a broken looking glass, and what little furniture there was, seemed as though it had been heaped together purposefully. Blood was running from beneath the door onto the garden path, and so dripping onto the road.

Other information recorded at the time on the cause of death was regarding the mother, Mrs Elizabeth Watkins, who was then aged forty. She was found in the garden with her throat cut. Upon examination, each of the children's bodies exhibited terrible wounds all more or less within the region of the throat or breast.

The Father, William Watkins was also found dead in the

garden with his head resting on a bed of flowers. His throat was also cut and his face covered with flowers – 'Sweet William'. Lying on his back, he was fully dressed with the exception of his boots. His stockings were clean, though there was blood spattered on his trousers, vest and shirt.

The small crowd that had gathered outside, had by now, doubled in size and the talk was about Mr Watkins: could he have killed his family and then cut his own throat? This was soon discounted due to the fact that there was no sign of a blood stained knife near the body of Mr Watkins. There was also talk from the crowd that a man asking for money was seen in Llangibby on the previous night, he was a stranger to the village. Also, Mrs Watkins had said to friends that she was very nervous living in the cottage, especially at night, and feared for the safety of her children.

Soon, the police arrived from Caerleon and Newport. The crowd was dispersed from the garden and surrounding area. Many appeared far too deeply distressed to utter a word, but the first true indication of what had happened was mentioned by one of the crowd when he pointed at the little white gate and said 'look, there's blood stains on the gate. The murderer must have left by this way.'

The police naturally asked many questions in the surrounding area. They made enquiries at Usk prison, which was just three miles away from Llangibby. They discovered that a Spanish prisoner and former sailor by the name of Josef Garcia had recently been released. Josef had just served nine months imprisonment for theft in Newport. Whilst in Usk prison, Garcia had been well behaved and had served his full sentence. On 16 July, the day of his release, a prison warder had been detailed to accompany Garcia back to Newport.

Usk prison as it is today

Whilst travelling through the small town of Usk, Garcia escaped and disappeared along the banks of the river Usk. A search was made but no trace of him could be found. The prison warders did not pursue Garcia too far, due to the fact that he had been a model prisoner and had served his full time. On 17 July, the day of the murder, several residents of Llangibby, reported to the police that a good looking, middle eastern type man was seen sleeping near the main highway to Newport. This was not far from the scene of the crime. A search was made, but now there was no sign of the reported man.

The inquest was held in the parlour of the *White Hart Inn.* Despite the roominess of this quaint, low-roofed apartment, friends and neighbours of the deceased had to remain either outside or in the comfort of other rooms at the Inn. The jury assembled shortly before noon. The first business after the coroner's preliminary address was to view the bodies. The jurymen had a good quarter of a mile walk from the *White Hart* in the hot sun, on a white chalk, dusty turnpike road in order to arrive at the scene of the crime.

The cottage seemed sinister now, even in the broad sunlight of the day. It was no longer an honest man's home but a location of terror. The sunlight that slanted through the roof, shone onto the corpses of the poor murdered children. The feet of the spectators who had hovered about night and day had trampled the garden. A small group of the more curious went up to the cottage with the jury and found the horrors spread out before them. The acrid odour of burnt flesh and rapidly

The bridge at Usk near the prison where mass murderer Joseph Garcia ran when he escaped and made his way to Llangibby to murder the Watkins family in 1878

The bridge at Caerleon, near Newport where Joseph Garcia was seen crossing on his way to Newport after killing five members of the Watkins family in Llangibby in 1878

decomposing bodies turned their stomachs. This was a spectacle, which would be imprinted on the memory forever.

The corpses, though mutilated, were still recognisable. William Watkins, once a handsome and powerful looking man, with dark whiskers was now hacked and gruesome. Eliza, his wife, being seven months pregnant, presented a distressing spectacle, seeing the children slashed and burnt in their bedrooms must have been the most traumatic of sights.

On 18 July, Josef Garcia was seen walking over the river Usk bridge near Caerleon and was followed into the centre of Newport. He was now the primary suspect for the crime. Constable John Tooze of the Newport Police Force was not sure if the man was Garcia or not and so he sought further assistance. PC Tooze went to the Monmouthshire Police Station in Bridge Street and asked for an inspector of that force to assist him. This agreed, the two men went to Newport's rail station approach. There they found the Spaniard drinking water from a fountain. Together they arrested Garcia.

Garcia was taken to a police cell on the right-hand side of

Bridge Street, formerly the Lyceum and currently a car park. He was questioned, charged at Newport police station and returned to Usk prison to await his trial.

At his trial, it was noted that Josef Garcia had been in possession of two large bundles of clothes and other items when arrested. The contents of these bundles were read out by the prosecutor as follows:

one pair of boots,
a black coat,
two silk handkerchiefs,
some stockings,
a small looking-glass,
a clasp knife (blood stained),
a wall clock,
a blood stained shirt,
a white bag,
a scarf.

The black coat was given to Mr Watkins as a gift by a former vicar of Usk. It was made by a tailor in the neighbourhood and altered to a sort of jacket with side pockets to suit Watkins. Mary Ann Watkins, the daughter of the deceased gave evidence at the inquest:

I am a servant with Mr Oliver Davis at Usk; I am the daughter of the deceased. On Monday last I was at home, I left home at 10 o'clock in the morning and went back to service. When I left home my parents were quite well, and my brother and sisters too.

Mary identified the white bag, produced, as bought by her mother, then the boots as her father's, also the trousers, black silk handkerchief, the black coat and the other items. The clock she last saw on the wall of her parent's cottage. There was also an un-cut loaf of bread in the house then, which she recognised as the one produced in court, the tin she last saw on Monday, the stockings having belonged to her sister and the scarf to her brother.

Mary's sister, Catherine, also confirmed all the items shown in court belonging to the family. 'I recognise them all, the stockings are mine. I was home last Sunday.' A number of other people in the Usk area gave evidence at the inquest that confirmed that the property found in Garcia's possession belonged to the Watkins family. It was established that the boots of the murdered man were found on Garcia's feet, also some of Mr Watkins' clothing.

The funeral of the Watkins family took place in the evening of 20 July at Llangibby church, an old fashioned white-washed building hardly more than a stone's throw from the scene of the murder. They buried the family in one deep grave, Father and Mother lying side by side with the three children on top. The churchyard is just behind the *White Hart Inn* in a quiet acre of tranquil countryside. The vicar of Llanbaddock performed the sad ceremony. Crowds poured into the church all day, especially from Newport. That same day the people of Llangibby felt the best thing that could be done would to raze the cottage to the ground.

Garcia was taken to Gloucestershire to stand trial, and was found guilty and taken back to Usk to be hanged.

The memorial stone for the Watkins family murdered in 1878, Langibby churchyard.

The Execution of Joseph Garcia at Usk

*The scene became one of terrible suspense as the hangman
stooped to draw the bolt;*

The local press reported the execution in some detail:

*On Monday, 18 November, we witnessed the closing scene of
the Llangibby tragedy, and the curtain has fallen forever over
one of the bloodiest incidents in the modern history of this
country. Joseph Garcia, the murderer of the Watkins family, is
no more; he has suffered the extreme penalty of the law at the
hands of the common hangman, and that he justly merited the
punishment is the verdict of the whole country, for that terrible
cry of vengeance which went up throughout the length and
breadth of the land on 17 July never abated in the slightest
degree, and now that Justice has had her sway, the feeling is
appeased. Yet, as an alien, every consideration was shown to
Garcia in order that he might prove himself innocent of the
dreadful crime laid to his charge, but during a period of four
months not one single fact was forthcoming to refute the strong
chain of circumstantial evidence which was adduced at the
tribunal presided over by Justice Bramwell, at Gloucester, and
to the last, he protested his innocence. During the time the
wretched man spent in the condemned cell prior to his
execution no steps were taken by those who interested
themselves in his behalf to enlist the sympathies of the public,
and not one palliating fact or argument in favour of mitigation
of the sentence of death suggested itself to the minds of any who
were acquainted with the revolting details of the murder, and
consequently no action was taken to obtain a reprieve.*

*Garcia, since his condemnation, conducted himself in much
the same manner as when he was undergoing imprisonment
for committing a burglary; he did not appear capable of
realising his awful position till within a day or two of the
execution. He did not take his food well of late; the only thing
he appeared to relish was beef tea, and on that he was
sustained. Senór de Uncillo, the Spanish Consul at Cardiff;
Father WA Liguorio Echevarria, a Spanish priest, of the
Carmelite Church, South Kensington; and Father Croft, the*

*Roman Catholic prison minister, paid several visits to the
condemned man during the last fortnight. On Saturday last,
Garcia was visited by John C. Hanbury, Esq, the High Sheriff
of the county of Monmouth; Edmund B. Edwards, Esq, the
Under-Sheriff; Senór T de Uncillo, the Spanish Consul,
Cardiff; and Senór de Angullo, the deputy Spanish Consul,
Newport. He was then formally given over to the executioner,
who arrived at Usk by train on Friday evening. The gentlemen
named, remained with Garcia for about a quarter of an hour,
and Senór Uncillo most solemnly asked him to tell the truth,
but he persistently stated that he knew nothing of the murder.
Senór Uncillo then thought that so many around him might
influence him not to speak truthfully, and at his request, all the
others withdrew, but when alone with the condemned man, he
only received the same answer as before.*

*On Sunday evening, Senór Uncillo and his deputy again
visited the miserable man, who was then fully alive to his
serious position. On the Consul and Vice-consul entering the
cell, Garcia advanced and threw his arms around the neck of
the former, weeping bitterly, and crying out, 'They are going to
kill me for what I have not done.' He repeated the statement 'I
have not done it!' two or three times; and said, 'Oh! My
mother and sister.' He embraced the Vice-Consul then as he
had the Consul on entering. After this affecting scene, the
Consuls were about to leave, when he cried out 'Do not leave
me.' Father Echavarria entered the cell just as they left. He
conversed with Garcia, and then prayed, endeavouring to get
him to make an open confession of his guilt, but to no avail.
The priest then, almost as a last resource, fell on his knees
before the wretched man, and fervently exclaimed. 'I entreat
you, for God's sake, tell me the truth;' and in order to still
further to move him the Spanish father actually bowed down
and kissed his feet. This scene was very affecting; there was the
holy man on his knees earnestly entreating the condemned
criminal to confess the truth and make peace with God in the
few short hours there yet remained for him to live. The solemn
petition failed to make any impression upon his hardened
heart, and the only answer he gave was, 'No, I am innocent.'
He embraced the priest before the latter left. He was attended*

through the night by Holroyd and Coward, the two warders appointed for the duty. He did not sleep at all, but was very low spirited and uneasy. Every hour, he was shown a watch, and informed that he was one hour nearer his doom, but to that he appeared very indifferent. On Sunday night he was asked if his money should be sent to his parents. He refused to sanction that, neither would he give his consent to it being handed over to anyone else, and he did not give any instructions whatever respecting it.

On Sunday it was made known to several of the congregation of the Catholic Church, Usk that Father Echevarria and Father Croft would say an early mass on the following morning, having the one intention, viz, that Garcia would die in proper disposition. Father Croft began his mass at five o'clock, and then assisted at Father Echevarria's. On the conclusion of the service the priests left the church, but returned again at six o'clock for a few minutes, after which they proceeded to the prison.

Shortly after seven a number of persons began to wend their way to the neighbourhood of the gaol, evincing, as usual, a morbid curiosity in what was about to happen. A number of men and boys climbed the tall trees at the rear of the prison, but no view of the scaffold could be obtained from any spot outside the walls. The officials and others then began to arrive, and at half-past seven our reporter and five other representatives of the press were admitted. They were ushered into a small room, where they entered their names in the gatekeeper's occurrence book. A warder pointed out some of the principal objects, the most conspicuous being the scaffold, which had been erected by some of the warders on the south side of the gaol. Marwood was standing on the platform, having just fixed the rope to the beam, attending to the little preliminaries, such as testing the rope and seeing that everything was in proper order for carrying out his repulsive work. The scaffold is of deal, and painted black, altogether a very ugly looking object. On being interrogated by our reporter; the executioner said the rope was eleven feet long, and Garcia would drop nearly eight feet. The High Sheriff and the other authorities inspected the structure on Saturday, when

Marwood was present, and the latter gave a lengthy exposition of his accomplishments in the hanging business, and the 'scientific manner' in which he did his work.

When the priests entered the gaol, they at once entered the condemned cell, but Father Croft soon retired. Father Echvarri administered the last Sacraments of the Church to Garcia, and after listening to some spiritual advice, he made his confession, but not of murder, although the priest used the most solemn means in his power to get at the truth, and he expressed his astonishment at the continued declaration of innocence by the prisoner. The Reverend Father said Garcia's greatest wish, like that of any other boy, was to see his mother, and the thoughts of never having another opportunity of seeing her face caused him intense grief. He requested the priest to write to his friends and beg of them never to come to England, for there were bad people here; it was a bad place altogether, and he did not like it at all. About five minutes to eight the warders entered and escorted the culprit to the pinioning cell, whence he was followed by the priest. On reaching the prison room Garcia betrayed great weakness. He did not understand the pinioning process, and thought it was there and then he was to suffer. He said to the father, 'I go now;' whereupon the latter answered, 'No, no, courage, you shall know the moment.' In the meantime Marwood had secured the culprit's hands to his sides with a stout cord. When all was in readiness the doomed man was raised on his legs, and the cell was quitted. The representatives of the press took up a position a few paces in front of the gallows, the church bell, which had been tolling the funeral knell for about twenty minutes, struck upon the ear in its mournful sounds, when the procession filed through the doorway by the gallows.

First came Mr C.W. Usherwood, the deputy governor; after him the culprit, with Marwood and two warders (Whiting and Powell) supporting the feeble and tottering steps of the unhappy man, literally lifting him onto the drop. The Reverend father Croft and Father Echevarrria ascended the scaffold, the latter holding on high a small crucifix. The Under-Sheriff, Major Herbert, Captain Herbert, Dr D. Boulton, the Reverend J. Cadwallader and five or six warders brought up the rear, *whilst the High-Sheriff and the Spanish Consuls witnessed the proceedings from the window of the visiting justices' room, which overlooks the scaffold. Father Croft, standing on the right of the culprit, read the Psalms 'Have mercy on me, O God,' and 'Out of the depths,' (L and CXXIX) in English, so that all present could join in the prayer if they wished. Father Echevarria said 'Acts of faith, hope, and love of God,' together with the Lord's Prayer and a few pious ejaculations in Spanish, some of which the culprit repeated with him. The Father was very anxious to go down the drop, so that he should be with Garcia in the momentary agony. The culprit presented a most death-like, sickening appearance; his formerly dark features had assumed an indescribable colour. He was dressed in a blue Guernsey, a pair of policeman's trousers, and polished boots, with a grey flannel shirt underneath the Guernsey. His legs did not seem capable of supporting his body; the warders held him up, while Marwood kneeled down and quickly buckled a leather strap around his legs. The executioner adjusted the rope 'scientifically' around the neck of the culprit, who did not speak, or even open his eyes. Father Echevarria stepped forward and held the crucifix to Garcia's lips, which he kissed twice, and uttered the words 'Jesu, Jose, Maria,' quite distinctly. Marwood drew a white cap over his face, and the priests and warders stepped back. The scene became one of terrible suspense as the hangman stooped to draw the bolt: the platform gave way with a crash, and the soul of Joseph Garcia, the murderer of William Watkins and his family, was launched into the great ocean of eternity. An exulting cry of 'He's gone,' was raised by the men and boys in the trees outside. This was exactly at eight o'clock.*

All present immediately advanced to the scaffold and gazed into the pit. Convulsive movements were observable for about two minutes and a half, and then the body remained perfectly still. It was horrible to think, when looking at his body, that Garcia passed away with an emphatic protestation of innocence; he clung with brute-like tenacity to the statement, and we are obliged to come to the conclusion that a more hardened scoundrel never suffered death upon the gallows. The black flag, with 'Justice' in large white letters, was immediately hoisted over the prison entrance. Marwood did not move from the scaffold, but continued to gaze unmoved at his victim. He entered into conversation with anyone who addressed him, and he said he attributed Garcia's quiet death to weakness, as he nearly fainted whilst he was being pinioned. He (Marwood) thought that Garcia, when replying to the priest on the scaffold uttered a word resembling 'Justice.'

The reporters then visited the condemned cell, in which the unfortunate man had spent his time since his sentence. Passing down the central court of the gaol, ascending a flight of steps, and walking a few paces along the corridor, the cell is reached. It is much larger than the ordinary cells, and has a southerly aspect, being lighted by two windows of thick glass which do not permit a view of exterior objects. In the right hand corner was an iron bedstead, on which Garcia slept, the clothes being folded up. On a small deal table opposite the door were the remains of the breakfast, consisting of a jug of coffee and three or four pieces of bread and butter. The culprit had scarcely tasted this; one piece of bread and butter had been partially eaten, but the coffee had been sparingly partaken of. On the mantelpiece were two small loaves and several books. These were chiefly spiritual works, such as Las Noches de Santa Maria Magdelena *and* Librito de Misa, *an illustrated book and very simple. Garcia was exceedingly fond of the latter, and he would sit for hours poring over the pictures. The other books were* Burn's Standard Series *and* Meditations *(in French). On Sunday night Garcia made presents to the male and female warders of the small religious books which Father Croft had kindly sent him during his confinement. When standing in the debtor's yard a warder pointed out the grave in which the body would be laid after the inquest.*

Marwood did not leave the scaffold until 9 o'clock, when, after life had been pronounced extinct by the surgeon, he delivered the body over to the authorities. An inquest was held before Mr E D Batt, coroner, and a jury composed principally of inhabitants of Usk, Mr Randolph, of Abergavenny, being foreman. After the usual depositions had been taken, the coroner and jurymen appended their signatures to the document, of which the following is a copy:

Monmouthshire to wit. - An inquisition, indented, taken for our Sovereign Lady the Queen, at Her Majesty's Prison at Usk, in the County of Monmouth, on the 18th day of November, in the year of our Lord One Thousand Eight Hundred and Seventy-eight, pursuant to the directions of 'The Capital Punishment Amendment Act 1868.' Before Edgar Dumareq Batt, one of the coroners of our said Lady the Queen, for the said county, on view of the body of Joseph Garcia, now here lying dead at the said prison, known as Her Majesty's Prison of and for the County of Monmouth, at Usk, in the said county, within the jurisdiction of the said coroner upon the oaths of the undersigned jurors, twelve good and lawful men, of the said county, duly chosen, and who being then and there duly sworn and charged to inquire for our said lady the Queen when, where, how, and by what means the said Joseph Garcia came to his death, do upon their oaths, say that the said Joseph Garcia was a prisoner in the said prison, indicted and convicted, at the last Winter Assizes held for the said county at Gloucester, for the wilful murder of William Watkins, and sentenced to death for that offence, and that judgment of death was duly executed and carried into effect upon the said offender, Joseph Garcia, for the said offence, pursuant to the said sentence, on the day and year aforesaid, within the walls of the said prison in which the said offender was confined at the time of execution. And the jurors aforesaid, upon their oaths aforesaid, do further say that this inquest is now here held on the view of the body of the said offender by the coroner, of the jurisdiction to which the said prison belongs, within twenty-four hours after the execution of the said offender. And that the body of the said offender, Joseph Garcia, now lying here dead, is the identical body of the said offender, who was so convicted and executed for the offence aforesaid. And that the said offender, at the time of his death, was a male person, of the age of twenty-one years, or thereabouts.

In witness thereof as well the said coroner as the jurors aforesaid, have to this inquisition set their hands and seals, on the day and in the year and at the place first above written.

Edgar D. Batt, coroner – J.C.Randolph, foreman – J.O.Nicholas – E.F.Gray – John Hagget – William Evans – Sidney Smith – George Mundy – C.Coles – John Williams – George Davis – James Jones – James Morgan.

The local reporter continues to provide us with details about the inquest, the life of Garcia and the Watkins family:

During the inquest, Mr Usherwood pointed out a peculiar spot on Garcia's head about the size of the top of a tumbler glass, which had been bald, but was then covered with very short hair, as if it had only recently began to grow. That gave rise to the supposition that Mrs Watkins tore it out in the struggle. We do not remember any remark made of it by the surgeon who examined Garcia at Caerleon on the day the inquest was held on the Watkins's. Had the hair been pulled off by Mrs Watkins it would have surely been noticed soon after his apprehension. Of the early life of Garcia very little can be gleaned. He was born at a small town called Puebla, in the province of Valencia, Spain. His parents are very respectable people, his father being a farmer. The family consists at the present time of three sons and one daughter, all of whom it is believed are living at home. It would appear that Joseph, until he was fifteen or sixteen years of age, was given to indolence – a characteristic of the Latin races – and after that he joined the Republican army, which was operating against the troops of Don Carlos, the pretender to the throne of Spain. That he was inured to scenes of bloodshed may be taken for granted. During that war some of the most dreadful ravages ever committed took place; Carlists and Republican trying to out-do each other in acts of violence and cruelty. It is not improbable that Garcia, when a soldier, took and active part in the ravages that were committed by the Republicans on 10 November 1878, after a battle in the country between San Sebastian and Oyarzun, when the Carlists were defeated. Loma, the Republican general, no sooner gained the victory than he ordered his men to burn the farm houses and villages, and at night the whole country was aflame. Scenes of pillage and murder were rife during the carrying out of that terrible order, and it has been said by an eyewitness that the ravages committed by Loma's army were far worse than those perpetrated by the Carlists. When Alphonso was proclaimed King of Spain desertions in the Republican army were very numerous, and it may have been at this time that Garcia took to a sea-faring life. He came to Newport in a Spanish vessel some time in 1877, and on 25 September in that year, he broke into the house of David Williams, at the parish of St Brides. Whilst he was purloining some articles of wearing apparel, Mrs. Williams came upon him, and she at first thought it was her son, but she quickly discovered her mistake when Garcia turned round and threatened her with a knife. He was arrested for this offence, and at the Quarter Sessions at Usk, on 16 October, sentenced to nine months' imprisonment with hard labour. During his time in prison his conduct was very good, but the confinement did not appear to have any salutary effect upon him, for no sooner had he returned to freedom than his innate desire for wrong doing got the mastery once more; like a panther he watched his opportunity, and with what result is too well known. The scenes of blood Garcia witnessed, if not participated in, during the sanguinary revolution in Spain must have hardened his nature, even if he had not naturally been vicious, so that his unbending to confess his guilt at the last is not to be wondered at.

The Watkinses

... killed, along with their parents.

The lives of William Watkins and his wife, up to 16 July last, do not appear to have been remarkable for any stirring events, and they spent their days industriously and contentedly. William Watkins came into this neighbourhood from Whitchurch in Herefordshire as a boy, and was employed at the Llandowlas, Hendrew, Rhadyr, Estarvarney, and other farms, but did not appear to keep his situations long, although he was a good workman. While in Mr Crump's service at

Estavarney, he became acquainted with Elizabeth Ann Jaspar, of Monkswood, and about eighteen years ago they were married at Caerleon, Elizabeth Jaspar being then a servant to Mr Gething of Penrose.

He then, for the third time, entered the employ of the late Mr. Warren Evans, as waggoner. Some time after leaving Llandowlas it appears that he found employment at the different farmhouses in the district, and he resided in the house in which he met his death. He, however, did not stay continually in that house, till the sad event happened, but moved to the Forest upper part of Llangibby parish. Here Watkins and his wife did not get on so well as when they lived in the house which has since become so notorious, work in the immediate neighbourhood being scarce. Mrs Watkins, while there, often expressed to her sister (Mrs Jones, of Monkswood) that she should like to go and live again in the old place.

Subsequently, Watkins made arrangements with Mr Morgan, of Cefn Llech, and went back to live in the cottage on the side of turnpike road. Here they appear to have lived very comfortably, Watkins being well employed, and his wife, by her industry, managed to make garden produce remunerative. There are three surviving children, one son and two daughters. The eldest daughter is in the service of Mr Oliver Davies, Usk; the second with Mrs Williams, of Llanwysk; and the boy with Mr Lewis, of the Park Farm, Llangibby. Charlotte, aged eight years, Frederick aged five and Alice aged four were killed along with their parents.

CHAPTER 6

The Risca Mystery
1878

The lower he got, the more obvious it became that it was, in fact, a man's body. It was naked and covered in blood.

Looking down from Machen Mountain into the valley, sometimes called 'the valley of the shadow of death', we can see from the summit a magnificent view of the small town of Risca. One side of Risca joins Newport and old Caerleon, the other borders Caerphilly, Cardiff, Penarth, St Mellons and the Monmouthshire low lands.

Risca is a small town on the west side of Newport with a population of just a few thousand, and those few thousand, still talk about what happened in 1878. What happened was the sudden death of a popular Risca man, and his death is still a mystery.

Isaac Britton, a collier and bachelor, was a modest lad; he was never involved in a fight or brawl, and would rather walk

The small town of Risca near Newport as it is today. The hills in the background are where the murder took place in 1878

the other way than fight. He was a quiet and peaceful man, friendly and mild mannered.

Over the years he had become friends with another local man by the name of David Harries. David was twenty-three, married with one child, and at that time an out of work collier.

On Monday, 1 July 1878, Isaac Britton called on David Harries to accompany him in a search for work. They left Risca together, bound for Machen, where there were several coal mines seeking employees. They were seen walking from pit to pit for most of that day.

On Tuesday, 2 July, George Britton, father of Isaac was concerned for the safety of his son, Isaac who had not slept in his bed that night and had still not arrived home by 10 o'clock that Tuesday morning. Mr Britton first made enquiries at the home of David Harries who informed him that they had been walking from pit-head to pit-head seeking work. By evening they were both exhausted and had fallen asleep for a few hours but when he had woken up, Isaac had gone.

Mr Britton informed the police that his son had not returned home and that he was trying to organise a search party to find him. A Mr William Matthews of Risca and PC Dowden went with a search party of nine men to find Isaac Britton.

They started out at about 10.30 am from Risca, and after covering both sides of Machen Mountain and finding nothing, they decided to search a number of disused pits in Black Vein Wood. There were twenty-seven disused pits in the area and it took some time. Late in the day, William Matthews looked down into a black, seemingly bottomless, shaft and thought he saw something. It looked to him like a man's naked body. He called to PC Dowden to say that with the aid of a rope, he would go half way down the shaft for a closer look. The lower he got, the more obvious it became that it was, in fact, a man's body. It was naked and covered in blood.

So it was that the body of Isaac Britton, who had disappeared in such a mysterious manner on 2 June, was found in equally strange circumstances. The thirty-three-year-old bachelor who had lived quietly with his father now lay distorted and white in a black pit.

At the Coroner's enquiry, William Matthews, in the company

of PC Dowden said 'We went with a search party of men from Risca to look for Britton. We started at about 10.30am and searched Machen Mountain but there was no sign of him, we went over and searched several pits, looking down them and letting hooks down on ropes until late afternoon.' Matthews continued. 'We came to an old pit in Black Vein Wood, close to Machen Mountain. I looked down into a pit shaft and saw something which I believed to be a body, I called PC Dowden to the pit and told him what I thought, I went down the pit some thirty odd feet and I found that it was a body.' He described the body, 'it was naked, and mostly covered in blood.' Sadly he said:

> *Everyone in the search party looked down the shaft, and each one became convinced that it was the body of Isaac Britton.' 'I descended into the pit by means of ropes tied around me, when I got there I asked to be pulled back up immediately. I found the stench from the body so bad that I was glad to be out of there. I took a drink or two and went back to the shaft and stood there looking down. I then went down the shaft of the pit three quarters of an hour later, I could see that there was no water in the shaft area of the pit. It was then that I managed to bring up the body and part of its clothing. He was as naked as the day he was born, the upper part of him was clean enough, and it looked as if he had been washed by rain. He was lying on his left side; his head was doubled up under his shoulders, as though it went down the pithead first. I had taken two sacks with me to wrap the body in; there were also some items of clothing down there. A Risca man, Aaron Crook helped me to draw up the body, I then made a third trip down to retrieve the clothes. There was a waistcoat, one shoe, a cravat, a shirt and trousers, the clothes were as though they had been rolled up together, his body was pressing against them. It looked very mush as if the clothes had been thrown down and the body flung down afterwards.*

William Matthews ended his statement.

At the coroner's enquiry, this mysterious report into the death of Isaac Britton caused quite a stir. There were several manifestations of feeling against David Harries; after all, he was the last person to have seen Isaac. Harries was detained until the conclusion of the preliminary enquiry. It was mentioned that there were no fewer than twenty-one disused pits in the Black Vein Wood, and the location of most of them, was by no means well known. 'Some of them are so covered with briars and brambles that an unsuspecting wayfarer might easily fall down one of them, and there remain until chance brought them aid' said the coroner. 'This is surely a dangerous state of things, and the only wonder is that there have not been a whole crop of fatal accidents in the locality.

Mr WH Brewer, coroner for the Newport division of the county had opened the inquest on Wednesday, 23 June 1878, at noon touching on the death of Isaac Britton, whose body was being held at the *Tredegar Arms Inn*. Mr George Duffield was the foreman of the jury. After the jury had viewed the body, the following evidence was given:

George Britton, Father of the deceased, said:

I am a labourer, living at Risca, I saw the body of the deceased when he was brought back from the Black Vein Wood, and I am satisfied that it is that of my son. I last saw him alive on the morning of 1st of July about ten o'clock. He was in the house then, he came in, washed his hands and face, put his coat on, and went out, he did not tell me where he was going, they left the door together, and I never saw my son again, I watched them go across the Graig, my son was in good health. They seemed to be friendly, Harries had been in the house before, I never heard them quarrel in my life. He did not generally tell me where he was going when he was going out in the morning.

Mr Britton continued his statement:

On Tuesday 2nd of July, I asked my neighbours if they had seen my son. They said 'no'. I went to Harries' house on Wednesday night, and I asked him where my son was. He told me that they laid down on top of the Graig, and when he had got up, the deceased was gone. I asked David where he left my son, and what he had done with him?' He said 'We came over the top of the Graig in the fields and lay down. We went to sleep, and when I woke up 'Ike' was gone. I said 'you are a fine fellow if you don't know where he's gone to.' He repeated 'When I woke up 'Ike' was gone, and I haven't seen him since.' 'Nothing else passed, I turned round, wished him good night, and went away. 'I live by myself, and when I go out, I lock the door and take the key with me, I cannot tell if anyone has called when I was away. I left Harries in his house; my son had been brought up as a collier, but he was out of work. 'He was given to drink?' the Coroner asked. 'Didn't he often get drunk?' 'It was not very often that I saw him come home drunk' said the father.

The coroner continued:

'He used to go over to Machen with a Mr Edward's cart, he was thirty-three-years-old?'

'Yes, that is correct, he knew his way across the mountain well.'

The foreman then asked:

'I did not ask Harries which way they went into the Graig, nor what spot they lay down, and for what purpose?'

George Britton replied:

'I don't know, I assumed it was to sleep.'

The coroner then proceeded to examine David Harries, the man who had been apprehended on suspicion of being in some way or another, implicated in the death of Britton. He was liberated to attend the inquest, as he said on his release, 'To give evidence, please God.' Protected by the sheltering arm of his legal adviser, the man told what appeared to be a very straightforward tale.

The enquiry commenced shortly after ten o'clock, with Major Herbert, the Chief Constable of the county in attendance. Mr A J Plews, solicitor, from Merthyr, watched the case on behalf of David Harries.

David Harries, collier, was the first witness to be called. He said, 'I live at Risca.' The coroner then informed the witness that he need not say anything to incriminate himself. Harries then said:

I will speak the truth, Sir. I remember going to Machen with

Isaac Britton on the 1st of July, it was five weeks ago last Monday. We were cutting a bit of grass there, both of us, that was between 11 and 12 o'clock, before dinner. After cutting the grass for about half an hour, he gave up, as the old scythe would not cut any more. We went to my father's house, and he cut a piece of bread and cheese for 'Ike', that is what I called him. On leaving Machen I met my mother, she gave me sixpence, and I also had sixpence for Isaac. Three shillings I had in my pocket already. My brother-in-law, George Harries, came along with us, we were called into the Royal Oak Inn, at Machen, and we had one jug of beer between the three of us. We got up, went to the bottom of the road, and parted with George Harries. We then went in search of work towards Machen, called into the Crown Inn and had two pints of beer, and then we went to Frwm Ishta Inn, I paid for three pints, and Master Frank Woodruff paid for another pint each, making half a gallon of beer, we left at half past three and then went to the Lewis's Arms, the landlord of which is a cousin of Isaac's, we stayed there all evening, we spent all our money and left. Isaac was not drunk, he could walk very well, when a man can walk, he's not drunk, he was just 'in beer.'

The coroner asked, 'Then you think that so long as a man can stagger along he is not drunk?

Harries replied 'that is correct.'

'That is the popular belief in this country,' said Major Herbert.

Harries continued:

After leaving the station, we went to the Rollers Arms, and had a pint of beer which someone gave us, on our way home Isaac said he would like to go to The Royal Oak. He could get a beer there. They were turning out, the door was shut upon them, Isaac asked them to stand half a gallon of beer, but they refused, and began wrangling with him. I went to them and said 'He's quite an inoffensive fellow' and asked them not to touch him. With that one of the crowd said, 'Anything you want you can have.' I was then struck down by a man named William Green, and two or three others also pitched into me, one of them hit me in a middling hard place, on the forehead.

They didn't strike Isaac. It appeared as if it was me they wantedthey wanted to have their revenge on. I broke loose and ran away, but went back after a while. I heard that they had turned upon Isaac and heard what they had done to him. And Isaac cursed them fearfully. After staying a bit, we went on our way towards home, and Isaac still cursed the men. He wanted to go back, but I said 'You would be very foolish, as you are already out of it.' We sat down in a field on the breast of the hill, and he talked about going off. He wanted to be down there so he could go off in the morning to the moors. This was on the Machen side of the mountain. It was raining very hard. I had lost my hat on the road. We went up to the stile and there, both of us sat down to sleep. I can't say whether Isaac slept or not, and I don't know what time this was.

The coroner: 'Give me the time to the best of your judgement?'
Harries said:

I should think it was about midnight, 12 o'clock. I don't know whether Isaac slept, but when I woke up he was gone, I called for him, but had no answer. It being very dark and wet, I looked around but did not find him. I went from there to a little shed at the bottom of the incline, to see if he had got into that to lie down somewhere in the dry, but I did not find him and made the best way home as I could. God knows what happened to him, only God knows.

Mr Plews requested the witness not to continue using those words. It was a very disagreeable phrase.
Harries said:

I spoke to Mrs Chivers on Wednesday, she asked me where I left Isaac, I said I had left him on the breast of the mountain, Mrs Chivers is the woman who said that my clothes were washed in blood, she told everyone that.

The coroner said:

To those unfamiliar with the locality and the additional mystery in which the discovery of the corpse in such a spot enshrouded the affair will not be readily understood, as there was no path leading to the pit where Britton's body was found. Whoever threw the body down there knew of it's existence, also we have earth samples taken from the bottom of the pit, and those samples taken from the body, which were entirely different, it suggests that the body was buried somewhere else before being dropped down the pit.

The coroner then continued with his summing up. He asked first whether the jury were satisfied with the evidence that had been brought before them. They had all the evidence that could be obtained, in his opinion, and he could not see how they could get any further evidence. Everything had been done that could have been done.

After deliberating for three hours the jury returned the following verdict:

We find that the body of Isaac Britton was found dead in a pit. We are of the opinion that he did not fall there accidentally, but that he met his death in a manner unknown before being thrown into the pit for concealment.

Even today the people of Risca sometimes stop and wonder why this mystery occurred, and why this murder remains unsolved. The murder happened 126 years ago, and some people that visit the area ask 'Is this the valley of the shadow of death?' The answer is no. Risca is a very pleasant place to live.

The hills just beyond Risca, where the body of Isaac Britton was found in a disused mine in July 1878

CHAPTER 7

Double Murder at the Tank Cottage
1909

... he [Police Constable Baile] *opened the door and discovered a most shocking spectacle.*

Silently, presumably in the dead of night, a dreadful crime was committed in a small property known as Tank Cottage, in Bassaleg, near Newport. The crime which sent a ripple of horror throughout Newport and the whole of South Wales, involved two elderly people, both of whom were found dead in their beds with their heads battered beyond recognition.

Bassaleg was a small and pleasant village on the very outskirts of Newport. Here, were two small two-storied cottages just a dozen yards from the main road. Charles Thomas, who was eighty-two-years-old, and his wife Mary, ten years younger, had occupied one for several years. Charles had worked for many years for the Tredegar estate, had served the first Baron as well as Viscount Tredegar, and for a considerable period, he had occupied The Lodge at the main entrance to Tredegar House. Owing to his wife's eccentricity, who in later years had declined to open the gate, they moved to Bassaleg and finally on to Tank Cottage.

On Thursday, 11 November 1909, Charles and Mary Thomas retired to bed at about 9 pm, something they had been doing for a number of years, often falling asleep with the light still on, which was noticed by neighbours and friends. Although elderly and limited in their activities, they were respected in the community and considered to be a nice, pleasant couple.

On Friday, 12 November, everything was quiet as usual at Tank Cottage. It was not until the evening that neighbours realised the Thomas' had not appeared all day and the bedroom light was still burning. The alarm was raised after the neighbours had tried knocking the door several times but had received no answer. Eventually, when Mr Harris, a baker from the stores at Pontymister, could not get his usual response, it was decided to contact the police.

Police Constable Baile, who lived a few doors away, was immediately on the scene and he decided to make a forced

entry. As he entered he called out in a loud voice 'Hello, Hello' but there was only silence. He made his way through the small house and on up to the front bedroom, he opened the door and discovered a most shocking spectacle. Lying in bed were Charles and Mary Thomas, their features battered almost beyond recognition. They must have been killed whilst they slept and it looked as though they had

The Pump House at Tank Cottage in Bassaleg, nr Newport in 1909, the only existing image of the building.

been bludgeoned with an extremely heavy object. Word got about, and everyone in Basseleg felt shocked by the news and felt a sense of dread when night fell and it was time to sleep. What sort of person kills someone asleep in the dead of night, and who knows if he or she would strike again?

By mid-morning, the whole of Newport had heard about it. By now, Bassaleg was crawling with police; house-to-house enquiries were carried out with most of the residents in the village. Everyone had to account for his or her activities on the night of the crime. Hundreds of people visited Bassaleg on the weekend,

This photograph shows Tank Cottage at Bassaleg, Newport where Charles and Mary Thomas were murdered in 1909 by William Butler who went to the gallows on 24 March 1910.

the recent developments, details of which were published exclusively in the *South Wales Argus* on Saturday, had aroused the greatest interest, and from early morning there was a constant stream of visitors from Newport, Cardiff and all the adjacent villages. Many people came on bicycles from more distant places and even wagonettes were used. Throughout the day, the enormous crowd stood in the roadway, gazing with morbid interest at the Tank Cottage. When the constables on duty, PC Nurden and PC Baile, happened to be looking the other way, people were plucking sprigs and cuttings from the bushes overhanging the garden wall as souvenirs of the horrible tragedy with which the place would always be associated.

On Sunday morning, police made a thorough search of the nearby river as well as adjacent streams, but nothing was found, no weapon, no article of clothing, nor anything that might have belonged to the old couple. A young porter at the Great Western Railway station at Bassaleg, named Pickering, saw a man whom he thought he knew in the vicinity shortly after midnight on Thursday 11th, and stated that:

> ...the man picked up and iron fishplate, he was a very short man, with a beard and he was wearing a small cap on his head, he also wore a coat – not a long overcoat, but a short one, he carried a large stick in his hand, a stick picked out of hedges and sometimes used by farmers and drovers, he was an oldish man and had a black beard that was turning grey. He was not black in the way a coloured man is black, but was very dirty in the face, as if he had rubbed something over it.

The police took note of this. It had been established that a window had been cut with a glass cutter next to the door at Tank Cottage, this, the police thought, was the way the intruder was able to break open the door.

Telephoning from Bassaleg shortly after three o'clock on Monday 15th, an *Argus* reporter said that the police had good reason to believe that in their search for the weapon, they were looking for a flat bar of iron, one and a half yards in length, about two inches wide, and one inch in thickness. The police representative was in a position to positively state that a piece of iron answering the above description had been missing since the latter part of the week. It was needless to point out that if the iron was used as a weapon it might have caused the injuries inflicted upon Mr and Mrs Thomas. The piece of iron in question had been missing from the garden of Mrs Baker, who occupied the cottage next to that where the crime was committed. Mrs Baker's cottage overlooked the garden from the window in the pine end of Tank Cottage. The piece of iron had been in the garden for over twenty years. It was used by Mrs Baker's husband in his work as a carpenter. Mr Baker had died some twenty years ago, and Mrs Baker used the iron for other purposes. The police also reported that:

> *This bar is now missing, and up to the present, despite the most energetic search on the part of the police, no trace of it has been found. It has disappeared in a wholly mysterious and unaccountable manner.*

The funeral of Charles and Mary Thomas took place on Tuesday, 16 November, the place of internment being Bethesda Chapel, The Cefn. The procession left Tank Cottage shortly after one o'clock, but long before that hour, people, whose feelings had been outraged by the crime, began to congregate opposite the cottage that had been occupied by the murdered couple. Many journeyed from, among other places, Newport, Castleton, Coedkernew, Rogerstone, Rhiwderin and Michaelstone. Several employees of the Tredegar estate and Tredegar Park had been granted the time to attend the funeral and they all followed the procession from Bassaleg to the Cefn. The Reverend TG James, pastor of Bethesda Chapel, conducted the service at the house and at the graveside. At all the houses in the village, and practically throughout the route, blinds had been drawn out of respect. Charles and Mary Thomas were taken to their final resting place.

Feelings were running high in Bassaleg as more information flowed in to the police and a number of people became suspects for one reason or another. One such suspect, known in the village as 'The Midnight Wanderer' was often seen walking around Bassaleg during the middle of the night. His name was William Butler, who lived in lodging with a Mrs Doody of Pye Corner, a small village about half a mile away. Butler, aged seventy-eight, still had a wife, but chose not to live with her. He was considered to be a kind and friendly man, but he did have a record for petty theft. This was not generally known. It was then that Bassaleg was hit by a sensational development: the police arrested Butler for questioning.

William Butler, hanged for murder in March 1910.

The whole village was staggered by this event. By now the police had firmly established that the motive for the crime was robbery. Drawers in a cupboard in the downstairs living room had had been ransacked and the contents thrown about in a manner which seemed to indicate that a most thorough and particular search had been made. A tin containing £150, the savings of the aged couple, was found intact in another downstairs room. The police also established that the murderer, had, in fact, gained entrance to the cottage by removing the pane of glass from a side window to the door and having put his arm through, could then pull back the catch. It had been noticed by neighbours that Butler was wearing a jacket with a rip or a cut at the top of the sleeve. This the police thought could have happened when the arm of the offender was stretching through the window to lift the latch.

Butler was interviewed by the police and was asked to explain how the rip or cut had occurred; they also noticed what appeared to be bloodstains on the front of his jacket. Butler said, 'If it is blood it must be from a pig that Mrs Doody, my landlady had killed.' Butler was then charged with the murder of Charles and Mary Thomas, but the police needed more evidence to firmly establish his guilt. Mrs Doody was contacted and said that although Butler lodged with her, he was not present on the day that she had killed the pig.

It was then that another sensational event was added to the tension in Bassaleg. A search was made of Butler's lodgings which resulted in the finding of an item that sealed the case. It was announced that among other things found in the possession of the prisoner was a glazier's diamond glasscutter. They added that, a pane of glass in one of the lower windows, near the door of the cottage occupied by the murdered couple had been cut using a glazier's diamond glass cutter.

It seemed there was sufficient evidence against Butler. He denied murdering the couple and at subsequent hearings added that he had had nothing at all to do with it. However, he was found guilty and sentenced to death. Butler was held at Usk prison until his execution. Whilst there, he wrote to his wife even though there was no relationship between each other. Writing on official prison paper, the letter read as follows:

Please tell me what has happened to Mr and Mrs Doody, as they do not reply to my letters. They know I did not do the murder as I went to bed at seven o'clock on the night and rose at the same time as she did on the Friday morning; and little Sammy can say the same. As for murdering poor old Charlie Thomas, I did not do it. I have done many kind turns for the old man. The people of Bassaleg do know who did do the murder. And they do know it is those ...(mentioning a name) Please reply.

Ever Yours

William Butler.

Butler, who had also used a number of other names, had an extensive criminal record. When sentenced, he created a dramatic scene in court as he attempted to strike an inspector and he hurled abuse at both the Judge and a witness, but on 24 March 1910, he is reported to have gone to the gallows quietly.

A street in Bassaleg today.

CHAPTER 8

Murder in a Cottage
1921

The gashes were so severe it was thought they might
have been made with a spade.

n 25 April 1921 the headlines in the *South Wales Argus* read:

MURDER IN A COTTAGE

CHURCHWARDEN BATTERED TO DEATH AT
LLANFRECHFA

ASSAILANT STILL AT LARGE

Llanfrechfa, is a very small village, less than three miles outside Newport. A very quiet and pretty place normally, but on 25 April 1921, all that changed. Another brutal murder – the third within the past twelve months – had been perpetrated in Monmouthshire.

On Sunday morning, the body of William Richards, aged seventy-three years, was found battered to death in an outhouse at the rear of Park Cottage, Llanfrechfa Lower. His head had been severely battered and bore terrible gashes; life had probably ebbed away one or two days before he was found. Park Cottage, prettily situated, nestled among the trees on the Llanfrechfa grange estate; it is approached from the Croesyceiliog to Caerleon main road by means of a small white gate. The path is narrowed by overhanging hedges and shrubs. It is a particularly dark and lonely spot once the sun has disappeared over the opposite hills and the moon often failed to throw its light through the tall leafy trees. The cottage itself looked out upon a broad expanse of mountains and valleys, works and houses, green fields and ploughed lands.

William Richards was busy at his usual work that Wednesday, stocktaking at Messrs Guest Keen and Nettlefold's Cwmbran works. He was absent from work on Thursday, but was seen in the garden as dusk fell that evening. It was rumoured that he had been in the neighbouring village of Llantarnam on the Friday afternoon. If true, then the murder would have been committed on that Friday night.

His body was found on Sunday morning, covered with hay, and lying in an outhouse. There were disgusting bruises and gashes all over the back of his head. The gashes were so severe it was thought that they might have been made with a spade. Walls inside the porch of the cottage were heavily splattered with blood. The body remained at Park Cottage whilst a constant stream of the curious passed by to watch the event unfold.

The approach to the cottage is one mass of green; the little white gate leads to a path with a roof of leaves. The front door is practically hidden from view, and all that can be seen from the highway, is a stone wall, relieved by two lattice windows. The cottage stands in a quarter an acre of ground, twenty yards from the dusty roadway. Apple blossoms faintly scent the air, and the trees and shrubs, bursting into green, speak of life – not a ghastly tragedy.

William Richards had worked hard for nearly three score years and ten; however, he still walked daily, with marked regularity, to Messrs Guest, Keen and Nettlefold's at Cwmbran, there to earn his daily bread. He was highly respected in the parish, where he held office as the people's warden at the parish church. He was a familiar figure to all who resided in the district. His wife had died many years ago, and his housekeeper, an elderly spinster, passed away on 19 March 1921. Richards was alone in the world, at least, he had no relatives within easy reach. His only comforts in his closing years were his work, his church, and his books. Long into the night, the day's toil over, William would sit reading. On the night that he was attacked, he had just retired to bed, clad only in a shirt, trousers and slippers. He answered a call of the night and opened the door to death.

A thin line of blue smoke rising above the trees, announced daily to the world that William Richards still lived, despite his seventy-three summers, the absence of that blue smoke announced his death.

The Grange was situated at the southern extremity of the Park Cottage garden, and Mrs Perkiss used to notice Mr Richard's chimney smoking each day. But for her observation, many more days might have passed by before the grim tragedy came to light. Mrs Perkiss missed the smoke and went to investigate, but when she entered the garden on the Sunday morning, accompanied by her son, Frank Perkiss, it was too late. William Richards was long dead. No gentle greeting awaited that neighbour and friend of twenty-three years acquaintance.

There was no development in the murder mystery on Monday morning, and by noon nothing in the shape of a definite clue had been obtained. The spade, with which the old man was thought to have been attacked, first with the flat blade and secondly with the edge, was blood stained. It was possible that this might provide the vital set of fingerprints which would help the police with their investigations. 'The fact that the crime is now some days old adds to the difficulties,' said the Chief Constable and Superintendent Barry, who were early visitors to the scene. There was little doubt that the motive for the crime was robbery. It was stated that when the body was searched, a sum of about 11 shillings was discovered in the victim's pockets, together with his watch chain, but the watch itself had disappeared.

A *South Wales Argus* representative, who visited the area, was informed that the perpetrator of crime was undoubtedly someone either living in the neighbourhood, or one who was well acquainted with the habits of the deceased. Someone had been aware of his great age and failing strength, and of the fact that he lived alone. The attack must have been swift and deadly, for no one heard screams, although there were three cottages within a distance of fifty to sixty yards.

A statement from the police involved:

Mr Richards was probably called to his cottage door, possibly strange noises had disturbed him, and he went to investigate. He went to the door to receive his visitor, and on the threshold of his cottage, he fell, the victim of a foul and unexpected blow. Blood spurted from his wounds and spattered the walls. Lifeless, or nearly so, he was carried, or dragged to the rear of the house. A trail of blood indicates the route of his last journey, a pool of blood discloses his temporary resting place. To cover up the deed, the front door was again locked, the key was taken away, and once again all was quiet.

As the lifeblood of William Richards drained away, and the neighbourhood slept, a candle on the kitchen table flickered its last, and burnt to the very end.

A few days later a lady noticed that she had lost a ten-shilling note whilst visiting the scene of the crime. She told her husband when she arrived home and they returned to Llanfrechfa to search for the missing money. Whilst doing this, Mr Howells' from Cwmbran, came across the key to the cottage in the long grass that was nearby. They had the key with prints, the murder weapon, but no suspect. Even now, after questioning everyone remotely connected to William Richards they have been unable to charge anyone with this heinous crime, but the case is still open, somewhere is a file labelled **Llanfrechfa Cottage Murder Mystery – unsolved.**

CHAPTER 9

Terror in Abertillery
1921

*It was beyond belief that the boy who was recently aquitted...
was again in the hands of the police.*

I n the small hilly town of Abertillery, to walk up High Street is like walking up a stairway to heaven; each step that you take becomes harder to achieve, but once you reach the top you are rewarded with outstanding and beautiful views of the valley below.

In 1921 the town took on a different image, all hell broke loose when the news spread that an eight-year-old girl had gone missing. For any parent this was the worst nightmare.

Young Freda Burnell of Earl Street, Abertillery, had been sent to a corn shop to buy poultry grit for her parents' chickens. It was on 5 February 1921 at nine o'clock in the morning that young Freda was told by her father, Fred

Below: Somerset Street, Abertillery today, where in 1921 the body of Freda Burnell was found at the rear of Mortimer's Corn Shop.

Inset: The corn shop store in the lane at the back of the corn shop (Mortimer's), on Somerset Street, Abertillery, in 1921.

Burnell, to wrap up warm and go down to Mortimer's Corn Shop on Somerset Street for some poultry grit and told not to be very long as it was a particularly cold morning. Freda set off, but by 9.30 had still not returned. Her father, Fred became concerned.

The streets of Abertillery were sparkling with frost and the town was very quiet due to the early time of day. Fred left home and made his way down to the high street. There, he asked one or two people if they had seen Freda. The response was negative, no one had seen her. He made his way into Somerset Street and arrived at Mortimer's Corn Shop. There he spoke to a young shop assistant by the name of Harold Jones to enquire if his daughter Freda had been in to buy poultry grit. 'Yes', replied Harold, 'she came in just after nine, made the purchase and left after a few minutes.'

Fred Burnell left the corn shop and spent the next few hours searching the streets of Abertillery but to no avail. The police were informed of the missing child and promised Fred that they would do everything they could to find her. Fred went home to inform his wife and family of the fearful news.

On Sunday, 6 February two members of Scotland Yard arrived and immediately began their enquiries. A mountain search took place, members of the town accompanied the police effort, but the search came to an abrupt halt when they received news that the body of a young girl had been found in the back lane of Somerset Street.

An intimate friend of the family said that he went into the lane at about 7.15 am At that time there was no body to be seen. Apparently the perpetrator of the crime saw him and hid behind a hedge. Afterwards, when the coast was clear, he climbed back into the lane and placed the body of the young girl across the path. Here, her body was discovered with her head against the wall of a storage shed, her legs were tied with string and her hands tied behind her back. A scarf had been tied around her mouth. 'The shed is the one used by Mortimer's Corn Shop, which is just there', said the family friend, as he pointed to the back of the shop.

The news spread rapidly of the discovery and Abertillery was filled with indignation and disgust at the brutal murder of the fair haired and innocent child. Groups of neighbours and passers-by gathered together to discuss the latest developments of the tragedy as it unfolded.

The headline in the *South Wales Argus* was:

CHILD MURDER MYSTERY, LITTLE GIRL OUTRAGEOUSLY AND BRUTALLY STRANGLED

The article went on:

The body of a bonny, intelligent, nine year old girl, Elfreda Elsie Maud Burnell, daughter of Mr and Mrs Fred Burnell, a collier, of 9, Earl Street, Cwm Cottage Road, Abertillery; was found early on Sunday the 6th of February in a narrow back lane in a thickly populated area, a few hundred yards from her home. The child had been outrageously and foully murdered and her assailant is still at liberty. On Saturday morning, after partaking of breakfast the child's father sent her to fetch a 10lb packet of grit and a packet of poultry spice from the shop of Mr.H.H. Mortimer, The Corn Shop, Somerset Street. The child was always prompt in fulfilling her errands, but as an added incentive, Elfreda was told she would receive a penny on her return. Gaily, and with a light heart she danced out of the house on what was to be her last journey. She reached the shop safely, she was served by Mr Harold Jones, an assistant, and paid him 2d for the spice. The tradesman had no 10lb packets of grit, and the child using her judgement, refused the loose grit offered, with the remark that she would first ask her mother if it would do, again she reached the street – and there she disappeared. So far no one has come forward to fill in the essential links in the broken chain. The next that was seen of the child was when her dead body was found at 7.30 on Sunday morning.

Police enquiries continued and it was soon established that Harold Jones, the shop assistant, had been the last person to see Freda alive. Harold was a bright young man of fifteen years of age, liked by most people. He had a good sense of humour, was a jolly person and frequently cracked jokes. He spent most of his time reading books and was learning to play the organ.

In his job as assistant salesman at the corn shop he was considered to be efficient, competent and capable of managing the shop without help.

Before approaching Jones more enquiries were made to a number of people from the Somerset Street area, a young lad of fourteen, named Levi Meyrick, who lived in Mitre Street, came forward with some important information that involved Harold Jones.

Meyrick told the police that he saw Jones between 10.20 and 10.30 pm on Sunday, 6 February, crossing the road near the Metropole Theatre. When he asked Jones where he was going at that time of night, Jones replied:

> Over to Mortimer's shed to get some potatoes to deliver in the morning and lock it up. We walked across Mitre Street, turned up King Street, then across to Princess Street, he turned into the lane where we arrived at the shed behind Mortimer's Corn Shop. Another lad by the name of Clisset had joined us. Half way down the lane Harold said 'You wait here while I go down to the shed.' Harold walked on alone, turned and whispered loudly, 'You lot keep quiet.' And that we did, Harold went into the shed and spent, I would say, about two minutes inside. When he came out, he locked the shed door and came back to us whispering 'Keep quiet, keep quiet.' Clisset asked, 'Where's the potatoes?' Harold replied, 'Still in the shed, I'll pick them up in the morning.'

The police were now convinced that they needed to talk to Harold Jones. Meanwhile, house-to-house enquiries continued, and virtually every male member of the community became a suspect. For the next couple of days suspicion and mistrust crept into everyone's lives, and virtually no one slept at night.

On Thursday, 10 February, a neighbour from Somerset Street came forward and told the police that on Saturday, 5 February at about 9.10 am that he was in his back garden when suddenly he heard an horrific scream which came from the area occupied by Mortimer's shed. The shed had boarded up windows and most people in the area knew that Harold Jones held the only key available. At the time the neighbour thought children playing in the lane had made the scream.

Harold Jones was arrested but denied having any involvement with Freda's death. At 10 on the morning of the murder, Jones, in the company of another youth, Frank Mortimer, made their way to the shed when Jones said to Mortimer, 'Frank, there's no need for two of us to go in, I'll get the potatoes, you go back to the shop.' Jones was the only known person to have entered the shed on the day of the murder. Jones was taken into custody and formerly charged with the murder of Freda Burnell.

Abertillery was completely dumbfounded, most people knew Harold Jones to be a kind and willing young man who loved music. It seemed impossible to imagine him harming anyone.

On 21 June 1921, Jones went on trial. In court, Deputy Chief Constable Lewis stated that the prisoner was charged with the wilful murder of Freda Elsie Maud Burnell on 5 February at Abertillery.

Chief Detective Inspector Helden said, on oath, that at 7.55 pm, on Monday, 7 March, with Detective Sergeant Soden and Deputy Chief Constable Lewis:

> *I saw the prisoner, Harold Jones, who was being detained at Abertillery Police Station. I said, 'I am Police a Officer, and I charge you with the wilful murder of Freda Burnell at Abertillery, on February 5th 1921.' Jones replied, 'I know it looks black against me, but I never done it!'*

Deputy Chief Constable Lewis said, 'On the evidence, I ask for a remand until tomorrow morning.'

Jones was then removed to the cells and as he was leaving the court his father shouted 'Keep a good heart boy.'

At 6.45 pm on the following Monday, after considering their verdict for over five hours, the coroner's jury returned an open verdict regarding the death of Freda Burnell. The coroner refused to accept this; he entered the courtroom with the unanimous verdict of 'murder against some person or persons unknown.' The foreman of the jury thanked the coroner for his courtesy, and in reply he said that they had brought in their verdict and he must accept it, and so Harold Jones left the court a free man.

Jones returned home to Abertillery having been found 'not guilty' of this dreadful crime. He was welcomed home by the town band and townsfolk. Balloons and bunting were on display and parties were going on everywhere, even the town officials welcomed him home. Obviously his happy character and warm personality had led everyone to believe completely in his innocence. Harold Jones was simply not the murdering type and the fact that there had been insufficient evidence against him provided an expected exoneration of his innocence. Soon Harold was back at work. Police enquiries continued to search for the killer, for if it were not Harold Jones, then who was it? The murderer was still at large!

On Friday, 8 July 1921, just two weeks after Jones had been acquitted, an eleven-year-old girl called Florrie Little was playing in the same street where Harold lived. Florrie lived at number 4 Darren Road and Harold lived at number 10. It was late evening and Harold had the house to himself. Looking through the front room window Harold noticed Florrie playing hopscotch outside. Jones went out and invited Florrie into his home. Unaware of any danger Florrie went up the front steps, through the doorway and into the passage. She was instantly strangled and dragged into the kitchen. Once there she was beaten over the head repeatedly with a wooden baton. Not

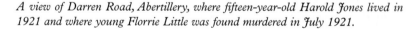

A view of Darren Road, Abertillery, where fifteen-year-old Harold Jones lived in 1921 and where young Florrie Little was found murdered in July 1921.

satisfied with this Harold Jones slit her throat with a very sharp knife, and then he lifted her over the kitchen sink for the blood to drain. Next he wrapped her body in one of his father's shirts and dragged her back through the hallway and up the stairs. Once there, he stood on a small table and lifted Florrie's body into the attic through the trap door in the ceiling. Harold quickly stripped off his clothes and took a bath. Alone in the house, and in the belief that all the blood stains had been removed, Harold went to bed.

Florence Little had lived only six doors away from the Jones house. Just before 10 pm Mr Little went into the street to tell his daughter that it was time for bed and to come home. There was no sign of Florrie. Mrs Little knocked doors and at number 10 Harold was asked if he had seen Florrie. His reply was 'No'. He said he had not seen her all evening.

A search was made of the streets in the district, when the news spread that she was missing, search parties were organised. They searched all night long to no avail. Under a great pretence Harold Jones joined in with the search and at one stage remarked 'As we're not finding Florrie, shouldn't we get in a team of blood hounds.' At 10.30, during the search Harold returned home with his father.At 11.45, father and son both joined the crowd to make a mountain search for the little girl. They returned home at 3.20 am without a sign of Florrie!

At 8.45 the following morning, PC Cox called at 10 Darren Road and requested a search of the house. Harold had left the house some time earlier. Whilst upstairs PC Cox called out to Mr Jones, 'Who sleeps in the bedroom with the trap door in the ceiling?' 'Harold, my son' was the reply, 'He's gone out somewhere.' 'I've found her body in the attic and I would like to talk to him,' said PC Cox.

Mr Jones left the house and made his way to Mitre Street where he found his son, to whom he said, 'Sonny, come on home, they've found the body in our house, it will be you or me that will have the blame, come up home and let's face it.' When father and son reached the house, Mrs Jones said ' Harold, my son, be brave, they've found the body in the attic.'

Abertillery was once again a town in mourning. For the second time within six months a little girl had been found brutally murdered and Harold Jones, the fifteen-year-old shop assistant, acquitted on 23 June 1921 of the murder of Freda Burnell, had again been arrested and charged with the latest crime. This time the sensation was nationwide.

When the news of yet another murder at Abertillery travelled the country, the information though scant, bare and crude, but not lacking in grimness, horrified them all. It was beyond belief that the boy who was recently acquitted of the charge of murdering Freda Burnell was again in the hands of the police.

The *South Wales Argus* reported:

> *The victim is Florence Little, aged eleven, the daughter of Mr Arthur George Little, a miner, of 4 Darren Road, Abertillery, and a playmate of Florrie Jones, the sister of Harold Jones in Darren Road, where both children lived. Florrie Little suddenly disappeared, and after an all night search the body of Florence Little was found at number 10 Darren Road by P.C. Cox in the space between the ceiling and the roof of the house occupied by Harold Jones and his parents.*
>
> *The evidence against Jones was overwhelming, beneath the kitchen sink, traces of blood were found, a wooden baton found clearly showed traces of congealed blood. Upstairs, blood was found on a small tabletop that was used to stand on, in order to place the body of Florence into the attic. The trap door leading into the attic also bore bloodstains.*

During the period before the trial, Harold Jones made two confessional statements. The first read:

> *I Harold Jones, do hereby confess that I wilfully and deliberately murdered Freda Burnell in Mortimer's shed on February 5th 1921. The reason for this act was my desire to kill.*

The second statement read:

> *I Harold Jones, do hereby confess that I wilfully murdered Florence Irene Little on July 8th 1921. The reason for this act was a desire to kill.*

Harold Jones was tried for the murder of Florence Little. The evidence was so overwhelming, his confession sufficient, that the jury found him guilty. He could not be hanged due to the fact that he was just fifteen-years-old. Therefore, he was detained at His Majesty's pleasure.

After serving eighteen years in custody, Jones was given the opportunity to be released to fight for his country. During the 1939 war, he joined the Royal Commandos. Afterwards he left the forces and took residence on the outskirts of Newport. There he tried to live a quiet life away from the glare of publicity that he achieved in 1921. He returned to Abertillery on one known occasion only.

In 1963, regular dances were held at Glasgow House in Abertillery, and many of the local people were more than happy to attend. One Saturday night the dance was in full swing when half way through a dance number the band faded out and stopped playing. The crowd wanted to know what was happening and turned towards the entrance door. There in the doorway stood Harold Jones, still recognisable despite the passage of time. He entered the room, so the band started to play again and the dancing continued. Not receiving much of a welcome, Harold Jones left the dance, never to return.

CHAPTER 10

A Murder that could have been Prevented
1924

... Dr Green went upstairs and made the discovery, the dead body being found under a matress with a severe wound to the head...

O n 15 March 1924, on a farm near Ross-on-Wye, a tragic murder occurred to a farmer's wife. Mr Thomas Stevenson took an axe from the garden shed and embedded it into his wife's head. His wife Mary, their son Ronald and Thomas had previously been a happy family, until Thomas became disturbed, suspicious and convinced that he was being poisoned.

Thomas and his son Ronald had just returned from a three month trip to Canada. On his return, he was hoping for a warm welcome from Mary. However, things did not seem to be the same as before the trip.

The small market town of Ross-on-Wye, where farmer Thomas Stevenson took an axe from his garden shed and murdered his wife Mary in 1924.

Here are parts of the transcript taken from the local newspaper:

'I have done it. I have killed your mother.' This was the statement made by Thomas Blakesley Stevenson, a retired farmer, or Croome Hall, Ponthill, near Ross, to his son. 'Now I will do for myself.' But the son snatched the knife away. The body of his wife was found underneath a mattress in the bedroom, with her head terribly battered. Medical evidence of the condition of Stevenson (who is now in custody on a charge of murder), was given to the inquest on his wife on Wednesday. He suffered delusions, and was under the impression that his wife was not pleased to see him back from Canada. He also thought he was being slowly poisoned, and steps were being taken to remove him to a private institution.

The inquest was opened at Croome Hall, Pentshill, near Ross, on Wednesday, by Mr OB Wallis, Deputy Coroner. The transcript continues:

'Mrs Stevenson, aged fifty, was found lying dead underneath a bed at her house, gagged with a scarf with her head terribly battered. Thomas Blakely Stevenson, the husband, who stands remanded on the capital charge, was brought from Gloucestershire in charge of warders.

Ronald Stevenson, the 22-year-old son, said he last saw his mother alive on 15 March 1924, and reported that she went upstairs to put her coat and hat on to go to Ross. He was working in the garden, and afterwards went into the house to get some dinner, and his father did the same. He did not think his father's retirement had preyed on his mind seriously. He was out in the garden about an hour, and saw his father coming up the garden path with a knife in his hand, holding his arms up. The knife (produced) was an ordinary table knife, and was quite clean. His father approached him surreptitiously. His father came near enough to touch him, and he took him down to the house. He did not struggle. Witness had stopped his father from committing suicide on the previous Thursday. He was then going to get a rope to hang himself. He found his father in the washhouse, took him out and locked up the rope. His father had threatened to commit suicide several times that month.

As he was taking his father into the house, he said, 'I have done it.' Witness asked him what, and he replied, 'I have killed your mother.' His father then raised the knife and said, 'Now I will do for myself.' Witness snatched the knife away, left his father, and went for the police. He returned with Dr Green and PC Bowen, and his father gave himself up. His mother had been to different doctors about his father's conduct, and there had been some talk about his father being sent to an asylum or private nursing home. Last August, witness and his father went to Canada in connection with the Canadian harvest scheme. They were away about three months, and his father seemed in good health. When they got back home, however, his father seemed to get depressed and got gradually worse.

Dr Llewellyn Green spoke to going to the house with the previous witness and PC Bowen. Stevenson gave himself up. In the bedroom a mattress was leaning up against the wall near the window. He pulled the mattress to one side and found the body of a woman lying under it. The face was covered with a shawl which he found was stuffed into the woman's mouth. On further examination, he found a large lacerated wound on the right side of the skull above the right eye and temple. Through this pieces of bone and brain matter were protruding. The woman was quite dead, and rigour mortis had set in. The wound was three inches long and must have been done with a heavy instrument, and the blow must have been tremendously heavy with weight behind it. On going downstairs he found an axe in the garden.

Dr Dunlop, Ross, said he had attended Thomas Stevenson since August 1922, when he was suffering from neurasthenia, but he seemed to have recovered. Witness had been attending Stevenson recently for depression and extreme insomnia. He was under the impression that his wife was not pleased to see him back from Canada. His mental condition deteriorated, and witness came to the conclusion that he was being slowly poisoned.

Witness had filled up forms for the man to be sent to a private institution, and he had arranged for Dr Campbell to examine him further in order that he might be sent to an asylum. The inquest was adjourned until 4 April.

The adjourned inquest on the body of Mrs Mary Stevenson, wife of Thomas Blakesley Stevenson, retired farmer, of Croome Hall, Ross, now awaiting trial for the murder of his wife was resumed on Friday, 4 April.

The principal witnesses were PC Bowen and Superintendent J Broad, of Ross, both of whom stated that Stevenson gave himself up; 'I have killed my wife,' adding, 'she is upstairs in the room on the right hand side. Stevenson also handed the key to the constable, and Dr Green went upstairs and made the discovery, the dead body being found under a mattress with a severe wound on the head, which, apparently, had been done with a hatchet.

Superintendant J Broad produced a remarkable letter the prisoner had handed to him at the police station on 8 March, in which Stevenson asked for police protection. On the occasion of that visit, said Superintendent Broad, Stevenson was accompanied by his wife and Thomas Ronald Stevenson.

Questioned by Mr Trevor Wellington, who appeared for the prisoner, who was present from Gloucestershire Gaol in the care of two warders, Superintendent Broad had said he did not think Stevenson had been to the police station before 8 March. He formed a definite impression on that occasion as to the nature of his complaint, and what he did was largely controlled by that impression. The usual thing in his experience when there was a question of certification was that the medical man in charge of the case made the arrangements for the getting away of such a patient.

He found upon the body of Mrs Stevenson, two certificates, one signed by Dr Dunlop, but the other was blank and possibly for the use of a second doctor. From inquiries made no second doctor signed or completed the second certificate.

Answering the jury, Superintendent Broad said when Stevenson came to the station with his people he could not interfere, nor had he any authority to take action to see that Stevenson was taken away. When brought to the station after the crime Stevenson said to him 'I am guilty officer', and when he told the prisoner that his wife was dead, he began to cry bitterly.

Thomas Ronald Stevenson, the son, recalled his father had

been an affectionate husband and father, and the only difference that had arisen had been out of his father's state of health during the last few months.

* Mr Wellington said with regard to the certification of the prisoner he was quite satisfied that everything was done by the relatives to get him certified, but owing to a series of accidents and illness of the magistrates, and the great hardships and great distress of mind, it was not done. There was no neglect on the part of the relatives.*

The jury returned a verdict of 'Wilful murder' against Stevenson.

The town of Ross-on-Wye today, home of Thomas Stevenson in 1924.

THE FARMER LOVED HIS WIFE

The Farmer

Canada's so big and fine
Mary would love it, I know.
Sometimes I miss her so very much,
I could simply get up and go.

I wish Mary could have been here,
She seems so far away,
But someone had to look after the farm,
She'll manage ok I pray.

Ronald and I are going home,
She's always been faithful to me.
Three whole months without us,
I wonder how lovely she'll be.

She looks the same, but quiet,
There's something on her mind.
I thought there'd be a welcome,
And this is all I find.

Dinners in the oven,
Everything's been done.
How could she cope without me?
And without our only son?

Perhaps somebody helped her,
Hanging around my place.
Looking at my woman,
I could smash him in the face.

Why aren't her arms around me?
Something is different, I know.
I might as well not be here,
I'll pack up my things and go.

I just can't sleep, I pace the floor,
Mary doesn't love me anymore.
I'm feeling sick, dinner tasted foul,
I'd rather be in bed than on the prowl.

The Farmer's wife

Thomas looks tired and thin to me,
Perhaps he didn't eat much over there.
I'll build him back up with mutton
And tender loving care.

He'll have to go to the doctor,
He hasn't slept well for weeks
His dinners on the back of the fire
And he's white about the cheeks.

His eyes across the table,
Bore into my soul.
His answers atmospheric
And his soup still fills his bowl.

The Farmer

What did you put in this gravy?
It tastes like something's bad.
Why don't you cook like you used to?
This is the worst I've ever had.

There's something wrong with this chicken,
And there's something wrong about you.
The porridge tastes likes poison,
And I don't think you've been true.

I wish I hadn't seen Canada,
Everything was fine before
I just can't live without her love,
I just can't live anymore.

Look at her asleep like a baby.
And me feeling sick yet again.
The weed killers low in the outhouse
And the doctor can't fix the pain.

I'll take the rope to the washhouse
And hang myself from the rafter.
That will end her poisoned food
And she'll be happy ever after.

The Farmer's Wife

Ronald must fetch the doctor,
He's suffering night and day.
I love him so much it hurts to see
My Thomas in such a way.

The Farmer

Look Doc I know there's something up,
Why don't you stay for tea?
Taste the cake and sandwiches,
And then argue back with me.

The son

My mother loves my father
My father loves her too.
I hate to see him down like this
But whatever can I do?

They say he has depression
And he'll have to go away.
I hear him at night pacing around
And he's lost in thought all day.

He's looking in our cupboards,
Checking receipts and bills.
Measuring the bottles,
And counting all the pills.

The Farmer

There's letters in her pocket,
She'll have me put away.
She's the one who should be locked up
I'll fix her up today.

Nobody believes me,
I know what your up to.
It won't be my lips honey
But yours that turn bright blue.

I'd rather remember you loved me once,
Than taste another dish.
You can keep your roast beef dinners
And eat your rotten fish.

Stuff your apple pie,
Pour your custard down the sink,
Swallow this scarf my little chef,
Your suppers truly stink.

You won't be boiling bones my love,
There won't be brains and cawl,
I'll hide you with the mattress
Because your cooking's foul.

Now there's nothing in the oven,
And you are finally free.
They would have put you away for years,
For trying to poison me.

CHAPTER 11

Murder in a Garden Chair
1924

Lewis drew his fingers across his [own] throat to indicate the action he was about to take.

In the small town of Blaenavon, a war widow called Mrs Joyce O'Keefe, lived at number 8 Cross Street which was a small cottage in a nice quiet area. Her husband, Edward, had been dead for a while, so, early in the year of 1924, Mrs O'Keefe made it known that she was prepared to take in a lodger. Money was short and her several daughters were all now married and living in other parts of Wales.

Eventually, a young man knocked the door and told Joyce that he was looking for accommodation. His name was Alexander Lewis. He was twenty-eight-years-old, a works labourer and a native of Leominster. Joyce put the kettle on and the two chatted away over a cup of tea. He seemed nice enough so Joyce agreed that Alexander could become her lodger.

Cross Street, Blaenavon, where at number 8 (now demolished) the murder of Mrs Joyce O'Keefe took place in 1924. She was found seated in a garden chair with her throat cut.

Part of Cross Street, Blaenavon today.

Joyce O'Keefe had a young son and four other children, it seemed a happy family environment and Lewis accepted his new home gladly. For a few months the relationship between Joyce and Alexander was fine. Lewis felt he had found his ideal home; he was a quiet man who enjoyed family life, and was always willing to help Mrs O'Keefe with any difficult jobs around the house. Lewis went to work each day whilst Joyce looked after the children and generally ran the home. There were also many visits from the grown up daughters and their families.

Joyce's eldest daughter was Mrs Catherine Brankley and when she and her husband visited, they suggested that Joyce should move to their house and live with them. Lewis had by now settled in, and although he had no say in the matter he did show an attitude of resentment. Some furniture was given to her daughter on 1 April on the understanding that it would be removed to her daughters home at Abertridwr until her mother would go to live with her parents at 39 Master's Houses, Coedcae, Blaenavon.

This action seemed to Lewis to mean that he would soon be homeless, and although he said nothing about it, his behaviour indicated that he was not at all happy with the situation. On Monday night, Lewis went to a boxing match in Pontypool, and arrived home at about 11 o'clock. Joyce O'Keefe was getting supper when, without any apparent reason, Lewis lashed out and hit Joyce's young son. Joyce protested that Lewis should not hit the boy without reason... Lewis then hit Joyce. Catherine, her husband and her father-in-law were staying overnight at the house and witnessed everything that occurred. Before anything could be done to stop him, Lewis then lunged at Catherine's father-in-law, who was sitting on a sofa holding a young baby. Lewis then challenged Catherine's husband to fight, he rushed into the kitchen, grabbed a poker, and a terrible fight broke out. Catherine went to fetch the police, but Lewis was so drunk that it took two police officers to calm him down. Once the police had left, Lewis remarked, 'After you lot go to bed there will be a murder in this house.'

Things settled down and everyone went to bed. On Tuesday morning, Lewis repeated the comment he had made the night before, 'There will be murder.' The others quietly ate their breakfast, but Lewis refused to join them. Instead he walked over to a birdcage, where he kept his razors. He took two and put them into his pocket, 'These will be across your throat today!' Lewis drew his fingers across his throat to indicate what action he was about to take. Later that morning, Lewis and the family were sitting quietly talking things over and Lewis agreed to be good. Catherine put her hand into his pocket and took out the razors, but Lewis did not know she had done so. She and her Mother then went out for a while and returned to the house at about one o'clock in the afternoon.

Lewis arrived home, and referring to the removal of the razors from his coat pocket said 'Yes you have been sly, haven't you!' For this he threatened to give Joyce O'Keefe a pair of black eyes, and rushed at her to carry out his threat, Catherine intervened and Lewis left the room. Catherine left her Mother alone for two or three minutes. When she returned, Joyce told her daughter that Lewis had come back into the room and had struck her in the face. At this Lewis put up his fist to strike Joyce again but Catherine stood between them and told Lewis to get out. 'I'll give you a pair of black eyes.'

Joyce had had quite enough and went out for a while. It was then that Lewis asked Catherine to give him his razor. She told him that she didn't have it. Lewis opened the kitchen drawer and took out a large army-knife, then he took the file out of the cupboard and began to slowly sharpen the knife. Catherine asked him what he was doing that for, and he replied, 'You won't give me my razor and I must shave.' She told him to go to the barber and offered him the money to get a shave. With that Lewis went berserk and became destructively violent, shouting 'This is my home. I live here too.' He put a poker into the fire, and when it was red hot he tried to sharpen the army knife upon it. He continued shouting and walking up and down the kitchen, threatening Catherine with every step he took. Next he tested the knife on a piece of wood. Apparently satisfied, he put the knife into his pocket, but refused to give any reasons for his actions.

Lewis began to ask where Catherine's mother was, and she told him many times that she did not know. She poured a cup of tea and he seemed to calm down. Between two and two thirty in the afternoon Joyce returned home and there was trouble immediately with Lewis rushing at her, pulling the knife from his coat pocket and shouting 'I will murder you, there's going to be bloody murder in this house, you'll see.' Joyce left to fetch the police but Lewis denied the threats and said that this house was like home to him and he was simply upset that he would have to find somewhere else to live. He told the officer that he had now accepted the fact that Mrs O'Keefe was moving house and that there was no place for him there. He also added that he would help Mrs O'Keefe to move the furniture out. With these assurances, the police left. Lewis seemed to be as good as his word.

The family began to load the furniture into the small van and Lewis helped them. He kept saying to Mrs O'Keefe 'Joyce, I want to speak to you alone, Joyce, I'm talking to you, I want a quiet word with you.' He continued to help with the furniture but kept following Joyce. 'I want to speak to you alone,' he persisted. Catherine asked him what he wanted to speak about but Lewis refused to tell her.

Later when Catherine and her brother were pushing the bedstead out, with Joyce helping, Lewis suddenly pushed Catherine's brother down the stairs and pushed Catherine flying into the corner of the room. Then he pushed Joyce on to the bed, which was lying on the floor, he pulled the knife out of his pocket and drew it along her throat, zigzag across her neck. Joyce wrestled herself free, she ran down the stairs and out through the back door of the house. She staggered to a garden chair still holding her throat.

Catherine and her brother rushed out into the garden and there was Joyce with blood pumping out of her throat. Overhead, Catherine saw a face at the window. It was Lewis upstairs who, after slashing Joyce's throat, had cut his own. He stared blankly down at Joyce, whose life was rapidly draining away.

The following Thursday a story appeared in the *South Wales Argus*:

BLAENAVON MURDER, WAR WIDOW'S ASSAILANT DIES IN HOSPITAL WITH TERRIBLE INJURIES

Alexander Lewis, 28, labourer, who has been confined at the Blaenavon workmen's hospital since Tuesday with self-inflicted wounds in the neck, after he had murdered Mrs Joyce O'Keefe, widow, 11 Cross Street, Blaenavon; with whom he lodged, died about 11.00 a.m. on Thursday morning.

CHAPTER **12**

There Were Three in a Bed
1926

He even played with them on the afternoon of the day
that he shot them.

Just four miles outside of Newport is a small village called Cwmcarn. Here, on Saturday, 2 January 1926, three little children were put to sleep forever and we will never know why.

The murder took place in the living quarters of the Cwmcarn Drill Hall; this was the Headquarters of the 2nd Battalion Monmouth Regiment. Sergeant John Breeze, aged thirty-six, lived in the Drill Hall Headquarters with his wife Mary and their four children. His son Ivor was fifteen, Iris was eight, Olive Mary was four and Betty Charlotte just eighteen months. There was a very limited amount of space for their living accommodation, so the four children slept in a bed in the kitchen.

Sergeant John Breeze worked as the caretaker at the Drill Hall and was responsible for weapons of war, which included a

The site where Cwmcarn Drill Hall once stood, where Sergeant John Breeze murdered his three children, on 2 January 1926.

Entrance to Cwmcarn High School, opposite the site of Cwmcarn Drill Hall that was the scene of the crime in 1926.

large number of rifles. Breeze, who had served throughout the 1914–18 war, was considered to be a war hero. Apart from brief periods of army leave, he was in France from 1914 until the cessation of hostilities. He had shown the utmost courage and daring on the battlefield including his part in the Battle of Ypres and at Hill Sixty, on 8 May 1915, he was amongst the 500 or so young men from Newport to fight. Only 129 of them returned home. It was there that Sergeant Breeze was recommended for a decoration for his gallantry.

On Saturday evening, 2 January 1926, Ivor, John's teenage son, went out for the evening, and so did his mother Mary, although not together. Later that same evening, John Breeze left home to visit his father-in-law, Joseph Harrison, who lived at 9 Feeder Row. When John Breeze returned home, he said to his son, 'Ivor, put your coat on and go and look for your mother, and if you don't find her, go to your aunts. Ivor went there, found his mother and ten minutes later, his father arrived. John Breeze sat down and told his father-in-law that he had lost his pipe somewhere. He talked about many things and seemed in no hurry to get back home. He borrowed a pipe from his father-in-law and was then contented. Shortly afterwards, mother, father and son left for home together.

On the walk, near the *Cwmcarn Hotel*, John Breeze put his arm around his wife's neck and said 'Kiss me Ann, don't go home, I have finished the children.' And with that Breeze turned away and walked off towards Abercarn. His wife called after him 'Come on back home and don't be silly.' Ann and Ivor could not appreciate the significance of the words they had just heard. John disappeared into the darkness.

Bewildered, Ivor and his mother looked into each eyes, but neither of them spoke. Hurriedly, they trudged their way over the rough lane, across the canal bridge, down a steep slope, then along an un-made track, which served as a road to the Chapel Farm, and on to the Drill Hall. They did not know as they were approaching their once happy home that it was now a house of death.

Both were scared to enter. John's words hung in the air, what did he mean? Ivor then plucked up enough courage, and leaving his anxious mother outside, he entered the kitchen. He lit a candle, and noticed a rifle on the table, which was not there when he had left the house. Ivor went over to the bed where the children slept but as his eyes were adjusting to the light, so he put his hand out and felt something wet. Looking at his hand, he saw that it was covered in blood. He shook the children, but was unable to wake them. Ivor went back outside to his mother, and together they went to a neighbour's house. The disbelief and horror of the situation made that Saturday night a very long one for Ann, Ivor and the neighbours.

On Sunday, 3 January, John Breeze returned to Cwmcarn and reported to the police at Abercarn Station. PC Morris was at the desk. He asked Breeze if there were any problems, to which Breeze replied, 'Yes, I suppose I shall be a guest for the next few days. I have killed my three children. I've shot them with a rifle: don't think I'm pulling your leg.'

A statement was made and read back to Breeze before he was asked to sign it. Breeze confirmed, 'I'm sorry to tell you that what you have told me is correct.' PC Morris then informed him that he would be arrested and held in custody. Later, in the presence of Superintendent Richards, Breeze was cautioned and charged with the wilful murder of his three children. Breeze then said, 'I'm off my chump, I must be mad,

I had no intention of doing them in, going up the road last night, above all, to my innocent little children, anyhow.' Breeze was committed for trial at Monmouthshire Assizes.

At the trial, in his defence, it was pointed out that it was not uncommon for soldiers that had endured some terrible experiences to become abnormal in later life. 'That is so' was the response. Psychologically, it is accepted that a traumatic experience can be repressed and sometimes break forth into some form of abnormal behaviour. The question to the court was whether Breeze had acted in that way on 2 January, because of some depressed emotion. It was agreed that this was most likely the cause. Although Breeze appeared to be normal there could be impulsive insanity. It seemed that Breeze had committed the acts of murder in a momentary lapse of sanity and the murders did not seem to be premeditated.

Anne Maria Breeze, wife of the accused, also known as Mary, was asked if her husband had any illnesses, to which she replied, 'He had complained that he was getting pains in the head, and occasionally, I had noticed him sitting very quiet. He was moody and complained about the headaches. Before the war, he was a bright, cheerful man. We were married for fifteen years.' Ann was then asked if she had, at any time recently, noticed anything abnormal in his manor or conduct. 'No, he would think for hours on times, and sometimes he would not answer me in the house. He was also jumpy at the least little thing.' 'Was the relationship between you and your husband happy?' 'Yes,' Ann replied. 'So you were quite happy, there was no trouble between you?' 'No, never,' she confirmed. 'I think your husband served throughout the war and had a distinguished record, but did he seem peculiar in any way after his return?' Ann informed the court that he was like he is now. After the Court hearing the Judge gave his summing up and the following was reported in the *Argus*:

> *The alleged confessed murder of his three little daughters, a gallant ex service man and respected citizen of Abercarn, Sergeant John Breeze, age thirty-six, faced a terrible ordeal at the police court of Abercarn on Tuesday, when he stood charged with having done to death his three well loved babies by shooting*

them in their sleep with a service rifle at midnight on Saturday January 2nd 1926. The accused man was alleged to have shot them on arriving home late on the Saturday night. Their dead bodies were found only a short time later by the accused's only surviving child, Ivor, aged sixteen, and later in the night the accused gave himself up to the police, and confessed to the terrible crime. A coroner's jury had already committed the accused on a charge of wilful murder, and the coroner, Mr D J Treasure suggested that Breeze could hardly have been responsible for his actions.

The evidence at the police court disclosed no new facts. The details of the occurrences on the night of the triple murder were told again – how the only son of the accused was sent to fetch his mother, and the father's confession to his wife on the road that he had 'finished the children;' his subsequent surrender to the police, also the discovery of the children's bodies.

Dr E M Griffith, JP expressed the opinion that the murders were committed during 'momentary impulsive insanity.' Breeze pleaded 'not guilty,' reserved his defence and was committed for trial at Monmouthshire Assizes. The judge and jury heard

'There Were Three in a Bed' murder at Cwmcarn on 2 January 1926. John Breeze, the father, murdered his three children. The main photograph shows part of the Drill Hall.

John Breeze

all of the evidence, but a number of witnesses were called to give further evidence on the state of mind of the accused. William Clutterbuck, a collier, knew the prisoner well. They had served together in the 2nd Monmouth Regiment. He was with the prisoner in the early days of the war. Of late he had noticed a change in his manner. On one occasion, the witness was talking to a man outside the *Cwmcarn Hotel* when the prisoner came up to him and said, 'Billy, I'm not going down there any more (meaning the Drill Hall) as the place is haunted.' Breeze also said, 'You and no other man will send me back.' Clutterbuck remembered the second battle of Ypres because it was the first time the Germans used poison gas, and his regiment was badly cut up. Breeze was there at the time, and they were both in the same platoon. Clutterbuck also said that Breeze had, on a number of occasions, complained of pains in his head, and on other occasions he had noticed him sitting very quiet.

The case was reviewed by the judge, who, in his address to the jury said, that owing to the way that the case had been conducted for the prosecution, it was entirely unnecessary to direct the jury. Nobody in the case had suggested that the man was not guilty. Counsel defending the prisoner, did not ask them to say he was not guilty. The jury could say that John Breeze was guilty of wilful murder or they could say that he was guilty but insane. Referring to the law on the question of insanity, the judge said that the law had been settled for nearly one hundred years. The jury ought to be told in all cases that every man was presumed to be sane and to possess a sufficient degree of reason to be responsible for his crimes until the contrary was proved to the satisfaction of the jury. This was especially necessary when the defence was on the grounds of insanity. It had to be clearly proved that the time the acts were committed, the accused was suffering from defective reason or disease of the mind, so as to not know the quality of the act he was committing.

'No doubt,' said the Judge, 'this man lived on terms of affection with his wife and family, and was fond of his children and played with them. He even played with them on the afternoon of the day that he shot them. It was an extremely painful position for the boy, Ivor Breeze, to give evidence, but he gave it extraordinarily well.' 'In this case,' the Judge continued, 'there is absolutely no motive whatever, and that, of course, pointed to madness. This was the work of a madman, and there is no alternative but for the jury to return a verdict of 'guilty but insane.'

The jury did not retire, and in a few seconds, returned the verdict 'guilty but insane.' They added that the prisoner was not responsible in law for his actions. The Judge ordered the prisoner to be detained during His Majesty's Pleasure. Breeze did not raise his eyes when the jury returned their verdict, and he showed no emotion as he was led from the dock.

The Cwmcarn, *where John Breeze spent a lot of his spare time.*

CHAPTER 13

The Shropshire Tragedy
1945

When he died he just weighed four stone.

A t a special magistrates' court at Pontesbury, Reginald Gouch, aged thirty-one, of Bank Farm, was charged on 9 January 1945, at Bank Farm, in the parish of Hope-in-Worhen, that he feloniously did kill and slay a child, one Dennis O'Neill, the son of Mr and Mrs T J O'Neill, of 88 Commercial Road, Newport.

Dennis, one of ten children, in the impoverished O'Neill family, was taken into the care of Newport Education Committee in 1939, after his parents were convicted of child neglect. Superintendent Taylor of the Shropshire County Constabulary said that after information of Dennis O'Neill's death had been received, the Director of Public Prosecutions was informed, and a warrant was issued for Gough's arrest. Police Sergeant McPherson said that after he arrested Gough,

The site of the house at the corner of Portland Street, where the O'Neills lived in the Pill area of Newport, in the early 1940s.

The opposite corner to where the O'Neills lived in the 1930s and 1940s, Portland Street, Pill, Newport.

and explained the warrant to him, Gough replied, 'There is no need to say anything, the evidence is wrong, and there is no need to say anything about it.' Superintendent Taylor asked for a remand in custody, which was granted.

On the same day, Mrs Esther Gouch, aged twenty-nine, the wife of Reginald Gough, was charged that on 9 January 1945, and on days prior to that date, at Bank Farm, having custody of Dennis O'Neill, a child under the age of sixteen, unlawfully and wilfully did expose the said child in a manner to cause unnecessary injury to his health. After the warrant for her arrest had been explained to her, Mrs Gough said 'All this is untrue.' Bail to Mrs Gough was granted, in her own surety, for the sum of £25.

Dr Davies of Minsterley, was called in by Mrs Gough to see young Dennis O'Neill. The doctor believed that he was called whilst the boy was still alive, but on arrival, he was dead. The doctor refused to provide a death certificate, and reported it to the police.

A school attendance officer, who gave evidence of identification, said the boy's parents were John Thomas O'Neill, a general labourer, and Mabel Blodwen O'Neill, of 88 Commercial Road, Newport. Acting on instructions from Newport Education Authorities, Victor Christopher Eastbury, of Christchurch Road, Newport, made arrangements for the boy to live at Bank Farm, in the nearby Hope Valley, in Shropshire.

Dennis and his brothers, Terry and Freddie, were in several care establishments before Newport Committee advertised for Catholic foster parents to take care of them. Harry and Doris Pickering of Pentervin, near Minsterley, took Freddie and also Terry for about a week, which left Dennis with no-where to go, and he ended up, on Mrs Pickering's suggestion, with Reggie Gough and his wife Esther, at Bank Farm, Hope Valley. Terry later joined him there, but behind the doors of the Gough's isolated hillside farm, the brothers were victims of appalling child abuse, suffering, neglect and violence.

On Monday, 12 February 1945 the *South Wales Argus* published the following front-page story:

PROSECUTION STORY OF THRASHING ON FARM

NEWPORT BOY BEATEN WITH FISTS AND STICKS

PHOTOGRAPHS OF BODY DESCRIBED AS MOST REVOLTING

AT TIMES THE BOYS WERE HELD LIKE PRISONERS AND PLACED INTO A DARK CUBBYHOLE

An extraordinary story of alleged cruelty to a Newport boy of thirteen by his foster parents was told at Pontesbury Magistrates' Court, when Reginald Gough, a thirty-one year old farmer, and his wife Esther Gough, were charged with the manslaughter of Dennis O'Neill, whose parents live at 88 Commercial Road, Newport.

Mr H Maddocks prosecuting, said a doctor found Dennis O'Neill lying dead on a bed in a room in shocking conditions. Photographs were taken, and it was obvious that Dennis hadbeen subjected to the most cruel and sadistic treatment. Mr Maddocks added, 'You will see pictures, they are the most revolting pictures I have ever seen, showing signs on his chest where he had been assaulted and signs on his back that he had been most unmercifully beaten. It is clear that he had been beaten by a man with his fists.'

The prosecutor then said, 'this is the most shocking case of neglect and calculated cruelty. It was said that on May 30th, 1940, an order was made by Newport Juvenile Court, committing to the care of Newport Council, Dennis O'Neil, Terrence O'Neil and a younger brother, Frederick, on the grounds that they were in need of care and attention, their parents having been previously convicted of offences against them in a case taken by the N.S.P.C.C. At first the three boys were taken to foster parents, on September 20th 1940, and remained there until January 6th 1941, then, because of illness of the foster mother, they had to be removed to another place near Leominster. It was intended by Newport Borough Council that the children should be left with Mrs Pickering, near Minsterley, but a hitch arose. Having made the arrangements, the Newport authorities learned, that without their knowledge, the proposed new foster parents had taken in a little girl, and were unable to take the three boys.

When a Newport attendance officer took the children to the place, he found that only two could be accommodated, and it was suggested by Mrs Pickering that the third boy might be taken to the Gough's farm, in Hope Valley, Terry later joined him there.

The case shocked the locals, including a one time school chum of the O'Neill brothers, Mrs Jean Adams of Callow Crescent, Minsterley, whose father had a smallholding near to the Goughs and their farm. Mrs Adams, now a mother with three grown up children said, 'Reggie Gough was a real hard case, but appeared to be a nice fellow and a good neighbour.' She continued, 'I blame the authorities. It was dreadful the way the boys were dumped with the Goughs.' Mr Maddocks said that Dennis was under-nourished and practically starved. No fat was found upon him, where a boy of that age would be expected to have fat, and there was none found on the body, only signs of unmerciful beatings. When the boys were taken to the farm, a lonely, isolated place, miles from anywhere, they were put to sleep in a bedroom in which there was just a bed, and nothing more, on the bed was a hard mattress, but as Terrence would say, no comfort. Bedclothes became shockingly inadequate during the bitterly cold winters.

When the two other children arrived, the O'Neill boys had to sleep on hard floor boards, Terrence would say they were promised another blanket, but never got it. The food, according to Terrence, consisted chiefly of three pieces of bread and butter and tea. Occasionally, they would get a piece of cake or apple pie, but when this happened, the number of slices of bread was cut down. 'These children were hungry,' said Mr Maddocks. 'They would get into the pantry and snatch a bite of anything they could find.'

Terence remembers they were often caught doing this, and were beaten for it. The state that Dennis got into can be appreciated by the fact that the boy used to crawl under the cattle and suck the teats to get something more nourishing. 'If Terence was right, the boy had to wash in a bath in the open yard, even in the bitterest of weather. Terence said that every night they were smacked on the hands, every night they had to recount to Mr Gough all the faults they had committed during the day, and received a smack for each one. He said he did not remember a single night upon which he and Dennis were not beaten. Terence used to have it on the hands and on the legs, but after a certain time, Dennis had it on the back. When Dennis went to bed that night, his feet were in a terrible condition, and he was obviously in great pain, Gough went to him three or four times and tried to stop him crying, and the last time he said, If you wont be quiet, I'll make you be quiet,' Gough put a lamp he was carrying on a shelf, put his knee on the bed, and banged Dennis with his fists. Dennis was lying on his back and cried out, 'Oh my back, oh my back.'

The following day Dennis died. Terence did not go to school, but was kept out of the way. That morning Dennis's breakfast was taken to the top of the stairs, and he was told, if he wanted it, he could fetch it. At one o'clock, Mrs Gough, rang up the doctor to say that Dennis had had a fit, but the doctor would say, that if he saw rigor mortis setting in, the boy had probably died between 9.30 and 11.30, that morning. The boy's story is a horrible one, a combination of the most shocking neglect and calculated cruelty,' said Mr Maddocks. a horrible one, a combination of the most shocking neglect and calculated cruelty.' Said Mr Maddocks.

Alfred Charles Hughes, surveyor to the Shropshire County Council, said that a 'Cubby Hole' referred to was 3 feet 3 inches wide and 6 feet 6 inches high.

After ten-year-old Terence O'Neil had given evidence in the Gough trial at Stafford assizes for nearly two hours, he burst into tears, and Mr Justice Wrottesley adjourned the court. 'He has done very well so far, but I think he had better have a rest, so he can answer everybody's questions,' said the judge.

Terence, with his fists clenched, had earlier demonstrated to a hushed and crowded court, how he alleged that Reginald Gough had thumped Dennis on the chest the day before he died. 'Mr Gough put his knee on the bed and was thumping Dennis with his fists on the chest,' he said. ' Sometimes we had a hundred stripes, sometimes fifty, sometimes twenty, very often the stripes were with a thin stick.' He added, 'Sometimes Mr Gough held up our hands, and gave us more. On one cold day, when the snow lay on the ground, he took off Dennis's clothes, tied him with a rope to a pig bench, and thrashed him with a thin stick. He hit him quite a lot.' When asked about the incident with the spinney, where Dennis had been sent for sticks, and because he didn't have sufficient, Mrs Gough had chased him out with a stick. The Judge asked what sort of weather was it? Terry replied 'There was snow on the ground, Dennis stayed in the yard crying. Mrs Gough threw her clogs

Terry, Dennis and Frederick O'Neill, photographed just before Dennis was found dead on a farm in Shropshire, January 1945.

at him, and told him to go back to the spinney. Dennis did not, but he went after Mrs Gough who told him she would tell her husband.'

Mr Maddocks asked, 'Do you remember something happening about a pig bench?' Terence replied that Mr Gough said he would put Dennis on the pig bench and thrash him. 'He put him on and tied him cross wards, and thrashed him, I was told to hold the lantern.' The judge asked, 'what did he tie him with?' the answer was, a rope. Terence was then asked by the judge, 'What clothes did Dennis have on?' 'He didn't have any, I think Mr Gough asked him to take his clothes off, but he would not do so, Mr Gough took them off him, and thrashed him with a thin stick, and Dennis cried.' The Judge then asked, 'I suppose you can't remember how many times he hit him?' 'He was hit many times, after the beating was over, Mr Gough untied Dennis.' Terence was asked by the Judge,' Do you know why Mr Gough punished him in that way?' 'I think it was because he had a bite out of a swede.' The judge's final question was 'Where was the swede?' 'In the cow shed I think,' was the reply.

The death of thirteen-year-old Dennis O'Neill caused a national outcry, which subsequently led to a public enquiry and changes in the law covering the care of children. It was considered, in both Newport and Shropshire, to be one of the most shocking child-killings of the century. The boy's ordeal ended on 9 January 1945, when his foster father beat him to death. When he died, he weighed just four stone.

At the end of the trial, Reginald Gough was sentenced to six years in prison for manslaughter. His wife, Mrs Esther Gough, was sentenced to six months. After surviving a dreadful start to their lives, the two remaining brothers, Freddie and Terence, worked hard to achieve a better standard of life.

CHAPTER 14

It was Murder in the Office
1946

*It wasn't until the film was over that his body was found,
slumped across his office desk.*

I n 1937 some major changes took place in Newport. One such change that made a difference to the Clarence Place area was the demolition of the Regal cinema. The cinema had stood there from the days of silent movies. It was a building that took pride of place and gave happiness to the cinemagoers throughout the town. The entertainment was first class.

The Odeon cinema, however, still stands on the corner of the East Usk Road and Clarence Place, although it no longer shows Hollywood movies. The atmosphere of the cinema in this period was electric. Depression and war had lowered the morale of Britain and there was more to come, but in the cinema, the world was a better place. The people who attended the cinema were temporarily lifted into a fantasy world, and those who worked there contributed to the suspension of

The Odeon cinema, Clarence Place, Newport, where in the 1940s Mr Parrington-Jackson was manager with a very happy staff. In about 1945 he was moved to the Odeon at Bristol and a year later he was found murdered in his office.

reality. It is much the same today; we enter the cinema, and forget our troubles for an hour or two. Trouble, however large or small, remains exactly where it was when you went in, and the staff, whose job it is to smile and entertain have troubles of their own.

The cinema was officially opened in 1938 with a parade of Life Guards on horseback, there were dignitaries from all over the country, and the people of Newport lined the streets to cheer and witness the event. There was also music from a military band. The Odeon was a dream cinema. Its Deco style and plush seating provided the perfect escape to luxury. It was warm and air-conditioned, lavish and sumptuously decorated. There were mammoth presentations on the huge screen, and in the evenings the manager, dressed in a frock-coat and white bow tie, would welcome the audience as they arrived in the capacious foyer: 'Good evening Sir, Madam, I hope you enjoy tonight's presentation.' Then with a big smile he would hand you over to a waiting usherette who, with a torch, would guide you to your seat.

The doormen were dressed in bright green uniforms, long coats, black belts, and rows of shiny brass buttons. There were a good number of usherettes ready to make your evening comfortable, they wore a similar version of the green uniform, with a short, full skirt. There was only one pageboy. He wore a pillbox hat at a jaunty angle, firmly held under his chin with a black leather strap. His jacket was short, with gold buttons and he had a wide gold stripe on the side of his trousers.

In the early Forties, a tall, handsome man, with film star features, black wavy hair and a scintillating smile, was appointed manager of the Odeon. His dress sense was impeccable, a black or white bow tie, together with a frock-coat, whatever the weather or time of day. He was so charming and amiable that he was liked by all of the staff. Most of his time was spent on the ground floor in the main entrance as if he was saying, 'I am here to welcome you, be my guest, have a wonderful time.' Robert Parrington-Jackson went out of his way to make your evening special, often shaking hands and paying a compliment to the latest arrivals. Mr Parrington-Jackson had an air of mystery about him. He had a slight

American accent, which was unexplained, and was thought to have come from the outskirts of London.

Part of his charisma, was his natural ability to interact with children and young people, and he was the first to welcome the concept of a Saturday morning Cinema Club for Newport's youth. The new event was called 'The Mickey Mouse Club.' There would be a selection of films for young people, and games on stage with participants selected from the audience. If it was someone's birthday, their names would be called out and the rest of the audience would sing 'Happy Birthday' to them. Mr Parrington-Jackson was always the main performer on stage when this event took place. Naturally, his warmth of character made him popular. To the children, he was like an uncle, and to the adults, a host.

On one occasion he was asked if he had ever been to Hollywood, to which he replied, 'Yes, I was in a film, *Robin Hood,* with Errol Flynn. I was one of his merry men!' He would then laugh and say 'See how merry I can be.' That would put a smile on the faces of the gang of children stood around him.

The Odeon was the only cinema to cater for the children of the town, so on every Saturday morning, hundreds of little boys and girls from every direction, would make their way to the 'Mickey Mouse Club.' Those children that remembered to wear their Mickey Mouse badges, received special 'star stamps' on their membership cards. Once inside, they were treated to a liberal helping of thrills and excitement. Films such as *Flash Gordon's Trip to Mars, Clancy of the Mounties* or *Tim Tyler in Ghost Town* were just a few of the spectacular shows. The children would scream with delight when the cartoons came up on the screen. When the games were over, the winners would help themselves to some goodies from the usherettes' confectionary trays. Before leaving for home, the club song had to be sung, at least twice. *There'll always be an England* was sung too, but the sound of *Every Saturday Morning* was always louder:

Every Saturday morning, where do we go?
Getting into mischief, oh dear no!
To the Mickey Mouse Club with our badges on,
Every Saturday morning at the O-Dee-On!

In the early 1940s the manager, Mr Robert Parrington-Jackson can be seen seated, centre of the photograph, wearing a white bow tie. His staff thought the world of him.

The happiness brought to Newport by the Odeon, under the management of Robert Parrington-Jackson was enormous, and almost unbelievable. Suddenly, and without warning, he was transferred to the Odeon in Bristol. He managed the theatre for just a few years. Nothing was heard of him during his stay in Bristol, he was just a part of happy memory. Then, one day in 1946, he made the headlines. Parrington-Jackson, manager of the Odeon, Bristol, was found murdered in his office.

It appeared that whilst the audience were watching a James Cagney film, which included a considerable amount of gunfire, someone had entered Parrington-Jackson's office and shot him at least twice under the cover of the film's soundtrack. It wasn't until the film was over that his body was found, slumped across his office desk. Who could have murdered such a popular man? Could it have some connection with him leaving Newport without saying goodbye?

After the police had made hundreds of enquiries in Bristol and Newport it was discovered that Robert Parrington-Jackson had had several romantic associations with his female staff. Apparently, he would, without any consideration for husbands or children, pressurise an usherette to come into his office to satisfy his considerable appetite. Although members of staff, and even some husbands complained, he had done nothing to control his desire, and would not release the women from his persistent pursuits. If an accusation was made, the accuser was simply sacked. On occasions, husbands and boyfriends would confront him, and the argument would become a punch-up, followed by the chap being escorted from the premises. So, it became apparent that Robert had another side to his character, and this was why he had been transferred. Perhaps it was because of the high number of involvements he had had that no murderer was found. There were too many suspects.

In the mid-nineties, a man that lived in the Caldicot and Magor area on the outskirts of Newport, wrote to the *South Wales Argus*, saying that his father, who was now dead, was a contract killer and was responsible for the murder of Robert Parrington-Jackson in the Bristol Odeon. Whether this was true or not, we shall never know. To the children of Newport Mr Parrington-Jackson was, and always will be, a kind and lovely man. If, today, one could stand in the auditorium of the Odeon cinema, you could very well hear the voices of a thousand children singing:

> *Every Saturday morning, where do we go?*
> *Getting into mischief, oh dear no!*
> *To the Mickey Mouse Club with our badges on,*
> *Every Saturday morning at the O-Dee-On!*

CHAPTER 15

When Bedmates Fall Out
1948

There was a pool of blood on the floor by her head...

Pontnewydd is a small district on the edge of Cwmbran, just a few miles from Newport. A Mrs Savina May Parry, aged thirty-two, of Wayfield Crescent, lived there. She was, according to neighbours and friends, a very happy and likeable person, married to John, with a son called Anthony. Savina was employed at the Caldicot lacquer factory, about five minutes walk from where she lived. Her work colleagues at the time would tell you that Mrs Parry was an attractive lady who always had something exciting to tell you and her stories were often amusing. Her neighbours believed her to be 'a very quiet woman.'

Mrs Parry left her home at 7.30 am on Tuesday, 8 June 1948 to go to work. Her husband John was working the afternoon shift at 'Guest Keen and Nettlefolds' as a steel worker. He left home before 2 pm and returned home just after 10.15 pm.

Street scene of Wayfield Crescent, Pontnewydd, near Cwmbran where Mrs Savina May Parry was found dead under the bed in June 1948.

When he reached home, Savina was not there. She always came straight home from work so Mr Parry went out to look for her. He spent the night searching Cwmbran but couldn't find her anywhere. On Wednesday morning at 9.45 am, he reported to the police that his wife was missing, and then returned home. A sergeant of Monmouthshire Constabulary was on his way to the house later that morning, when he met Mr Parry who had some dramatic news. John Parry told the constable that he had looked into every room and searched the garden after returning home from work the previous evening. He continued to tell the constable all about his search through the streets of Cwmbran during the small hours of the night and that he had not found her anywhere. Near to tears now, he went on to say that he had just found his wife dead underneath a single bed in the box room!

More police were invited to Wayfield Crescent and also a Professor J W Webster, who was the Home Office pathologist. Professor Webster would examine the body. Mrs Parry was lying underneath the bed, only partly dressed and her head was covered with several items of clothing. There was a pool of blood on the floor by her head, a spanner was resting upon the body and there were blood splashes on the walls and on her clothes. One garment was stuffed tightly into her mouth; her watch had stopped at 4.30 pm. Savina Parry was a small woman, being just 5ft 2 inches in height, there was a considerable amount of blood over her body and stuck in the blood on her thigh was an unused

Clifford Wills, who was hanged at Cardiff Prison for the murder of Mrs Parry in 1948.

condom. The gag was a child's coat, and it was discovered that over eleven inches of the left sleeve had been pushed well into the back of her mouth which had caused her tongue to hump. Her lips were punctured and bruised, she had a double black eye, and her neck bore pressure marks. There were three stab wounds in the left breast caused by something like a dagger. Professor Webster said that the stab wounds were the terminal act of bringing about the victims death. There were twelve individual splittings of the scalp, which were caused by a blunt instrument; also her nose had been broken. One of the stab wounds had passed straight through the heart. Mrs Parry had died from the effects of shock and haemorrhaging from the multiple lacerations to the head, stab wounds to the chest, partial asphyxia due to manual strangulation and that she had died in the afternoon of the previous day sometime before four o'clock.

Police enquiries on the spot were under the direction of Detective Inspector R Atkins of Monmouthshire CID.

The *South Wales Argus* were informed that the police were anxious to interview a man who knew Mrs Parry and may be able to help them materially in their investigations.

On 10 June 1948, from information received from friends and neighbours of Mrs Parry, a Clifford Godfrey Wills was arrested and charged with the murder of Mrs Savina May Parry. Mrs Parry and Wills had had an intimate association over a period of three years; sexual intercourse having taken place regularly during their relationship. On 8 June, the day she was murdered, Mrs Parry went to work as usual. Soon after midday, a colleague took her a light meal and at about five minutes to two she noticed Mrs Parry was preparing to leave the factory. As far as was known, with the exception of the accused, no one ever saw her alive again.

In the afternoon of the day on which the body was found, police went to the Wills's house and found Clifford Wills in bed. Drawing back the bed clothes they saw that Wills was wearing a shirt that appeared to be bloodstained, and they also noticed that he had a slight injury to the back of his right hand. He was cautioned by Police Sergeant D Plummer and asked to give an account of the bloodstains and the injury. Wills'

Clifford Wills leaving his house on being arrested for the murder of Mrs Savina May Parry, of Wayfield Crescent, Pontnewydd. 1948.

explanation at first was that he had been involved in a fight at Newport. Asked when he last saw Mrs Parry, he replied 'We were together in Newport yesterday and went to the cinema together, she has been mine for the last three years.'

He pointed out the clothes he had been wearing. The officers thought he seemed rather drowsy, and Sergeant Plummer asked him what he had taken. Wills said that he had taken between fifteen and twenty sleeping tablets. He was taken immediately to the police station and then to the hospital for treatment. Afterwards he was returned to the police station where he made the following statement:

> *She told me she would be ready to go to Newport just after 2 pm. I went to the Pontnewydd Hotel and had a drink. I called at Mrs Parry's house at about two o'clock, she had on a new look two-piece, which I had not seen before, we arranged to meet at the Romany Café in Dock Street, Newport, but she did not turn up. I waited a short time, and while I was waiting I saw a girl named Doris. I had spent the previous Saturday night with her and we were on intimate terms, I arranged to meet Mrs Parry, but she did not turn up.*

Later Wills then said, 'She had an appointment with someone, and I got a bit mad and decided to end it all, but I did not kill her sergeant.' He then asked, 'Did she suffer much?' A police officer replied to the effect that she had, and Wills added, 'She deserved to die.'

The same evening, at Pontnewydd Police Station, Inspector C Parsons told the accused he would be detained pending further investigation. Wills replied 'Our sex life was perfect, if I did not go to her, she would come to me.' Whilst being taken to Pontypool, Wills asked the police officers, 'What does it feel like to sit next to a killer? You've got your man.'

Early in the morning he expressed a desire to make another statement, which was alleged to have read, 'I have known Mrs Parry about three years, ever since I was demobbed. We became very intimate and lived for one another. She had everything a person could have, a home and a husband. I tried to break this association on several occasions.' A police officer asked 'What association?' to which Wills replied 'The association with Mrs Parry.' Then he added 'She was very friendly with my mother.'

Clifford Godfry Wills was committed for trial at the Monmouthshire Assizes, where the magistrates decided that there was sufficient evidence to warrant sending the accused man for trial at a higher court. It was mentioned that, in the

Gwent Police leaving the house where the body of Mrs Parry was found in June 1948.

event, Monmouthshire Assizes at Newport, in the Autumn would probably be the most suitable court.

Wills refused to admit his guilt but the evidence was overwhelming. There was positive evidence of identical blood groupings on his suit, and on his shirt with that of the victim. There were fingerprints in blood on Mrs Parry's handbag and a print of his shoe in blood on the bathroom floor. More fingerprints belonging to Wills were found on the bathroom walls.

Wills appeared before Mr Justice Hallet and denied all charges; however the evidence was too great and Wills was found guilty and sentenced to death. In 1948 the abolition of hanging was a sensitive political issue and Clifford Godfrey Wills was confident that hanging would be abolished. He made the remark 'well they won't top me!' Even when the Judge placed the black cap on his head and pronounced the death sentence by hanging, Wills seemed unmoved. On 6 December 1948, Wills was led to the scaffold in Cardiff prison.

CHAPTER 16

Body in a Reen at St Brides
1954

*He failed to get hold of him and stood back in horror when he saw
the murky waters of the reen turning red with blood.*

Like most other towns or cities, Newport has had its
fair share of unusual, prominent or noticeable
characters. People, who were, for some reason or
another, considered to be different from the majority. Newport
also had one or two people who were eccentric in their
behaviour or manner of dress. An example was a newsvendor
that suffered from a complaint that would prompt him to burst
into song or begin to dance about in the high street. Without
any warning the passers-by would see his newspapers fly into
the air and land on the pavement. Naturally, he inspired both
humour and sympathy. These days, with a larger and more
varied population we have become accustomed to unusual
dress and individual styles of fashion. Being individual now is
hip, then, to stand out from the crowd was non-conformist.

So it was with a Somali man that lived in Newport,
sometimes in lodgings or sometimes on the streets. His name
was Daher Gass and he was always dressed quite outrageously.
He wore house slippers, rain or shine, together with a light,
long smock that went down to his ankles with a frilly hem on
the bottom. He did have an overcoat, which was sadly worn
out, but his crowning glory was a gold coloured, heavily
stained, tea cosy, which he wore on his head! Daher Gass spent
his days wandering around Kingsway and Cardiff Road areas
of Newport. He was a loner who never attempted to make
conversation with anyone other than himself.

Hardly a mile away from newport on the North side of the
town stands a small village called Llantarnam. It was the home
of Mr Granville Jenkins, a forty-five-year-old married man with
a nine-year-old son named Howell. Jenkins worked for a
Gwent-based company called 'Guest, Keen & Nettleford' in

Cwmbran. He was employed by them as chief pay clerk and had been with the company since the age of fifteen, thus completing thirty years of service. Jenkins had the heavy responsibility of handling huge sums of money for the firm. He was happy with his work but always looked forward to the weekends for a complete change of activity, achieved by assisting his cousin Edward Nicholas.

Nicholas ran a small farm, called Penypare, in Cwmbran upon which Granville was only too happy to help. Nicholas had bought a horse without actually seeing it beforehand. The transaction was made with a farmer that lived in Pencarn Lane, also known as the 'Belt', near Duffryn, St Brides. This location is on the South side of Newport. The Belt was basically a long and narrow country road with a stream running alongside it, and was situated in a very lonely and remote part of the countryside. The whole area was divided up by streams and reens, which flowed across the flat plains from the Bristol Channel's high tides. A 'reen' is a local word used to describe the small rivulets of water that are filled with weeds, grasses and overgrown foliage. This part of Newport was frequently flooded, at times, up to four foot of polluted water swelled the banks and covered the nettles and brambles. This scenery, although quiet and tranquil, was unsuitable for walking in and would never be able to support houses; it was of course too dangerous to venture into.

On Saturday afternoon, 10 June 1954, Granville Jenkins accompanied his cousin Edward Nicholas to Pencarn Lane, Duffryn. They were to collect the horse that had been purchased by Nicholas sometime earlier. Together they travelled to Newport by van, arriving at about 2.30 pm. It was a bright, sunny afternoon and Jenkins enjoyed the journey. The van pulled up at the farm in Pencarn Lane at approximately 3.20. Nicholas got out of the van and was greeted by the farmer who was looking after the horse. After some conversation Nicholas waved to his cousin to leave the van and join them. He did so, and the horse was brought out of its stable. It was indeed a fine looking horse and Nicholas congratulated himself on having made a fine purchase.

The tailboard of the van was lowered and Jenkins led the

horse towards the vehicle, but the animal pulled away time and time again. After many failed attempts to get the horse into the van, both Nicholas and Jenkins became hot and frustrated. The more they tried to get the horse into the van the more stubborn and difficult it became. In the heat of the day, with tempers frayed, Nicholas went to ask the farmer for help. The farmer suggested that the horse should be taken to another farm further on down the road because they owned a ramp that would solve their problem. Jenkins was to lead the horse down the Belt towards the next farm. This was about a mile-long walk. Jenkins set off, holding the horse by its halter, knowing that the next farm had a solution to their situation. Besides, it was a beautiful day and the countryside was glorious. The lane was quite narrow with a rather wide reen on the right hand-side, which was about eight to ten feet wide. The depth of the reen could not be fathomed, as it was overgrown with weeds, but it was in fact six foot deep in places. Jenkins, with the horse at his side went on down the lane.

Meanwhile, Nicholas waited a while for Jenkins to make some distance before getting into the van to follow him. Nicholas thanked the farmer for his help and said goodbye. He drove very slowly down the lane, so as not to catch up with Jenkins. Before he arrived at the farm with the ramp, Nicholas was surprised to see the horse coming back up the lane in a gallop. There was no sign of Jenkins. Stopping his van, Nicholas got out, gabbed the halter and managed to bring the horse to

The scene of the crime, a lane in the Belt at St Brides, near Newport, where the body of Granville Jenkins was found.

a halt. After tethering the horse to the van he began to walk down the lane calling out for his cousin on the way. Perhaps the horse had bolted, but why? Surely his cousin would be able to call back, but there was no answer and Nicholas walked on in the silence. The stillness and solitude of the lane made Nicholas feel uncomfortable for if Granville had dropped the horse's halter he should have run after it – 'Granville, Granville' he shouted … still no reply.

Further on down the lane Edward Nicholas noticed something on the bank of the reen. As he approached he saw that it was clothing of some sort. He then spotted a canvas bag underneath the clothes and an old raincoat under that. None of this belonged to Jenkins. Picking up the raincoat Nicholas called out again 'Granville are you there?' The silence was broken only by the sound of his own voice. A few yards away he saw one slipper, Nicholas bent down to pick up the slipper from the edge of the bank, and there before him was a sight that made him jolt. Lying face down amongst the weeds and muddy water was his cousin Granville Jenkins. 'Oh my God'

Victim Granville Jenkins of Llantarnam.

exclaimed Nicholas as he reached down to pull Granville onto the bank. He failed to get hold of him and stood back in horror when he saw that the murky waters of the reen turning red with blood. At this Nicholas turned and ran back to the farm to get help.

Breathless and tearful, Nicholas, with great difficulty managed to tell the farmer of his terrifying discovery. The farmer immediately telephoned the police. In no time at all nearly thirty police officers from the Monmouthshire Constabulary arrived, and the investigation began.

First, Jenkins body was pulled out of the reen, a man's jacket was wrapped around one leg and it was established that the jacket did not belong to him; Granville was still wearing his own jacket. Blood poured out of the body as the water drained from his saturated clothing. Police photographers arrived at the scene of the crime and then the body was taken back to the farmhouse.

The jacket was searched for clues in order to establish the owner's identity and amongst some of the items found was a national insurance card that was wet and mud stained. The name of the owner was written in ink, which had just started to run. The name was D Gass. Police still searching the reen for further clues found a tea cosy floating just beneath the surface of the water, which was recovered and held as a possible source of evidence. The tea cosy was deep gold in colour with stains embedded into the fabric. This was the third piece of evidence that might lead to the murderer's identity. One of the police officers recalled that a man of a foreign nationality regularly walked the streets of Newport wore a tea cosy perched on the top of his head as if it were a crown. Also he wore slippers on his feet and his name was Daher Gass. The news spread like wildfire and the hunt was on for the murderer.

Neighbouring police forces were informed of the incident at St Brides and that they desired to interview the only suspect: 'Daher Gass.' Painstaking searches of the area took place but there was no sign of Gass. After a few hours a railway signalman telephoned the police and said that a man answering the description of Gass was seen crossing the main London to Cardiff line. Policemen and tracker dogs immediately went to the area, but there was no sign of Gass. Police encircled the crime scene by a few miles, in the hope that the suspect had not gone too far and would be flushed out of hiding. Eventually a police officer noticed a figure hiding in some long grass and brambles. As soon as Gass saw the police officer, he made a run for it.

Gass ploughed through reens and brambles, jumping streams and falling into them on some occasions during the chase. Other police officers joined in the pursuit. Despite being barefoot, Gass outran the police for over half an hour, when suddenly he stopped and stood still, much to their surprise. Gass unloaded from his back a small haversack, which he had been carrying. The haversack was thrown into a reen together with a large bladed knife; he then ran off again, but this time the police had gained distance and were beginning to close in on him. Inch by inch two police officers came within a few yards of Gass. The three men came to an abrupt halt, winded and exhausted, and Gass suddenly turned towards the officers. He was dripping with muddy water and covered in weeds, shaking, he pulled out a sheath knife and waved it towards the two officers.

Closing in on Gass, PC Dixon of St Mellons approached him with caution and said 'Come on, give yourself up.' But Gass just pointed the knife at Dixon who then shouted 'Don't be a fool Gass.' The knife continued to wave. By now, more police officers had arrived on the scene, and at this Gass stood upright and tossed the knife into the air. The sunlight lit the blade for a moment before it sank into the green depths of the reen. Dixon, now only a yard away, sprang forward with his handcuffs, but Gass did not resist as he was led away.

Gass was cautioned and taken to Risca Police Station where he was left to dry out, clean up and wait. He spoke very little English, and it was difficult to make any sense from his answers. The following day, a mine detector was used by the police to search the bed of the reen near the 'Old Belt' road at St Brides. A large machete knife, the size of a butcher's cleaver was discovered. It was confirmed by pathological examination that Granville Jenkin's injuries were most likely to have been inflicted with the weapon. Gass was charged with the murder, to which he replied 'Me kill nobody.' His clothing was sent for examination to the South Wales and Monmouthshire Forensic Laboratory in Cardiff. Blood of the same group as Jenkins was found to be upon them and Gass was committed to trial.

At Monmouthshire Assizes, Gass was found guilty of wilful murder and was ordered to be detained in Broadmoor at Her Majesty's Pleasure. Twelve months later, on 5 October 1955 Gass was released from Broadmoor to be returned to his native Somaliland on condition that he was never to set foot in this country again. This was a brutal and unprovoked murder, as Granville Jenkins was a peace-loving man and there seemed to be no motive for his murder. The decision of the Home Secretary to release Gass and return him to Somaliland was, at that time, inexplicable and shocked those police officers involved in the case. Jenkins was murdered by an eccentric maniac who might be ready to kill again in his homeland, God forbid it!

CHAPTER 17

Sudden Death in Dock Street
1959

He lay slumped over a pile of periodicals,
with two wounds to the head.

Dock Street, Newport, in 1959, was a street that stretched almost the entire length of the town, starting at the Old Green near Newport Bridge and castle ruin. The street was filled with small and large shops, pubs, a cinema, a fire station, the town museum, library, market, another cinema called the Olympia and the Town Hall. The further you walked down Dock Street, the quieter it became.

On Thursday, 19 February 1959, a thick fog descended over the already cold streets of Newport. At 5.55 pm Mr Wilf King walked into a newsagent and tobacconist shop and discovered the owner, Mr Gus Roberts, lying dead. He lay slumped over a pile of periodicals with two wounds to his head. After spending

Gussie Roberts' shop in Dock Street, Newport. scene of the crime in 1959.

the whole of Thursday night making enquiries, detectives were able to follow a definite line of investigation into the murder of sixty-five-year-old Gus Roberts of Dock Street, Newport.

Mr Roberts, known as 'Uncle Gus' to the local children, was battered to death in the back room of his shop at about 5 pm the previous day. Newport police began piecing together the events during a crucial five to seven minute period before Uncle Gus's murder took place.

Uncle Gus Roberts was a bachelor who lived a quiet and modest life, over the top of his very popular newsagent, sweets and tobacco business. He was very generous to the children who lived in the area, sometimes giving away sweets or providing fireworks for bonfire night to those families who could not afford them. In summertime, Gus would organise outings to the South Wales seaside, he charged nothing. For adults, Gus often extended cigarette supplies on a 'pay when you can' basis.

Gus Roberts's generosity fuelled a rumour that he was a very rich man. It was believed that he kept hoards of money at the back of the shop. Gus himself added strength to this rumour by occasionally boasting of his eligibility as a wealthy bachelor. In reality, although Gus's income was reasonable, he actually led a rather sparse existence, brewing tea in a very old kettle and eating his meals from an enamel plate.

Gussie Roberts (centre), a bachelor, who lived a quiet and modest life. He resided over the top of his newspaper shop in Dock Street, Newport. Gussie was very generous to the children.

On Friday, 20 February 1959, the *South Wales Argus* headlines read:

DEFINITE LINE ON 'UNCLE GUS' MURDER. ALL NIGHT ENQUIRIES INTO NEWSAGENT'S KILLING

After spending the whole of Thursday night making enquiries, detectives were today following a definite line of investigation into the murder of 65-year-old newsagent, Gus Roberts of 36 Dock Street, Newport. Mr Roberts, known as 'Uncle Gus' to the children he befriended in the district, was battered to death in the back room of his shop at about 5.00 p.m. yesterday. 'I see no reason to call in Scotland Yard', Newport's Chief Constable, Mr F.H. Smeed told the Argus.

Newport Police are piecing together a picture of what happened in the shop during a vital five to seven minutes. This was the margin of time to which they had narrowed down the time of the murder. Detectives believe that an 11-year-old girl, Janet Briggs, who lives in the area, may have been the last person to speak to Mr Roberts. She called into the shop at 4.55 on Thursday afternoon to give Mr Roberts a message from her father, Mr Earnest Briggs, of nearby Union Street. At 5.05 p.m., Mr Wilf King walked into the shop and found Mr Roberts lying dead with two head wounds and slumped over a pile of periodicals. There was blood everywhere. Mr King, a bricklayer of Fotheringham Place, Newport, ran into Dock Street for assistance. Two men followed him back into the shop, finding that Mr Roberts was dead, they summoned the police.

The police arrived and took possession of a bloodstained metal bar about a foot long, which they handed over to be examined by forensic science experts. The body of Mr Roberts had not been removed from the shop, which was now being guarded by two police constables.

At about 1.15 pm on the day of the murder, a man called Mitchell met a man called Pumford in Newport town centre. They talked for a while and then decided to go for a drink. First they went to a pub called *The Neptune*, 37-38 Dock Street, and then to the *Ruperra Arms* in Commercial Road.

There they met a man named Jones. The three men stayed in the pub until closing time. At 3.30 that afternoon Jones and Mitchell said goodbye to Pumford but almost immediately met another man by the name of Shaw.

Later that evening Jones and Mitchell split up and went their separate ways. Jones spent a few hours in the Maindee cinema on the east side of Newport and Mitchell continued on his pub-crawl.

That same evening, a barmaid at the *Griffin Inn*, Newport, said she saw Mitchell with relatives in the public house early in the evening of 19 February, 'He was having a drink and singing the song *Hang down your head Tom Dooley*. The second line of this song says 'tomorrow you are going to die'. Jones was not with Mitchell, and Mitchell seemed to be buying drinks all round and dropping small change on the floor as he did so.

Detectives still investigating clues in Gus Roberts' shop and back room found small change, copper and silver scattered over both rooms. They also discovered that the shop till was not working and were told that it had not worked for several weeks. Gus had been using a large Oxo tin as a cash box. The police searched the premises thoroughly but the Oxo tin was nowhere to be found.

A neighbour informed the police that two young men were seen looking into the shop after which they crossed the road and entered a very narrow lane called Tabernacle Lane which led to the back of the Tabernacle Church in the town's main Commercial Street. Later the same men were seen standing against the wall a few yards down the lane, looking towards the shop.

At 7.50 that evening Clement Shaw arrived at Newport Police Headquarters with some vital information:

I was walking up through the town and then on into Dock Street, a man named Mitchell pulled an iron bar out of his pocket and went to hit me in a joking way. He said 'How would you like a clout with this?' I put my hand up to push it away, and then he put the iron bar back into his pocket. Then Mitchell said 'Do you fancy doing a job?' I did not answer and walked away down Dock Street.

Shaw was thanked for the information and with that he left the Police Headquarters.

Immediately the police began extensive investigations and their thoroughness paid off, for just twenty-four hours after the murder, Newport detectives arrested Henry Mitchell, aged twenty-three, of Upper Cwmbran and George Jones, aged twenty-six from Newport. When Detective Inspector Jack Jones charged them with the murder at 10 pm on the Friday night, Jones was alleged to have said 'Yes, he done it, Mitchell, I seen him do it.' Mitchell said 'I do not want to say any more to what I have already said.'

At a special sitting at Newport Magistrates' Court on Saturday morning, both men appeared in the dock in Number 1 Court accompanied by four police officers. Also in court was the Chief Constable of Newport Mr Frank Smeed. Chief Inspector Mr Leslie Evans applied for a remand in custody and the presiding Magistrate, Mr J T Rice Edwards, duly granted this.

Later, Detective Inspector Jones spoke to Mitchell and Jones in the presence of Detective Sergeant Wade. Inspector Jones said to Mitchell 'I have reason to believe that you were in possession of this iron bar in Dock Street yesterday afternoon. It was found in Gus Robert's shop close to the body.' Mitchell said 'I have never seen it before, I have not been near the shop, and I don't know what you are talking about.' Later Mitchell asked, 'Can I have time to think things over by myself?' He was left alone for fifteen minutes, then he made a statement as follows:

I have thought things over and this is the truth. Me and George went into the shop. I went up to Gussie and grabbed the tin with the money. Gussie went to grab it off me, George came at the side of me and hit Gus with the iron bar.

After Mitchell had completed his statement he agreed to go with Inspector Jones to indicate where the money was. Inspector Jones continued, 'He took us to a spot underneath the Kingsway Viaduct in the centre of town and there pointed to an Oxo tin which was covered over with a piece of plywood which was resting against a bridge support.' Mitchell said

'That's the tin.' 'I cautioned him and took possession of the tin and found it contained a quantity of loose change. I later counted the money which amounted to £2-11s-3½p.'

Next, George Jones was asked to make a statement, he said:

At about 2.45 on the day of the murder, Mitchell and I were in the Ruperra Arms, Mitchell asked me where he could get an iron bar. He went on about getting some money for beer. I told him he could get one from the Old Town Dock if he wanted one. I went with him to the dock. He found an iron bar from some waste ground. We walked to the top of Dock Street where Mitchell pulled out the iron bar and said 'I would not like to be clouted with this, would you?' We then saw Shaw who was asked by Mitchell if he fancied doing a job. Shaw said 'No.' and left us. Mitchell and I went and stood outside Gus Robert's shop and found the door locked, Mitchell knocked on it and said 'If he don't come out I will bust the door in.' We went into the alley-way opposite the shop and waited there and then Roberts opened the door. We hung around for a few minutes then Mitchell walked over to the shop and I followed. Mitchell went into the little back room that was filled with bundles of newspapers and walked up to Gus who was sitting by the fire, there was a scuffle and I heard Gus shouting and moaning 'Please don't do it, don't do it.'

The statement added that Jones then came out of the shop and met Pumford, and that ten minutes later Mitchell ran past and said 'I'll see you later.' Jones said that after leaving Pumford, he went to the Maindee Cinema on Chepstow Road. Both Mitchell and Jones denied using the iron bar to kill Gus Roberts.

When the trial began on Monday, 8 June 1959 at Monmouthshire Assizes both men faced a charge of capital murder for which the death penalty was in force. Both men pleaded not guilty. The jury of ten men and two women were sworn in whilst Mitchell and Jones sat in the dock, each between two prison officers. Mr George Baker opened the case for the prosecution with a speech lasting one hour and ten minutes.

This was the trial that would make legal history, as Newport

Assizes was the first court in the land to try a case after the Homicide Act of 1957. This provided that if two or more persons took part in a murder, only the person who struck the fatal blow would be guilty of Capital Murder, and that any accomplice would be guilty of non-capital murder. The law was changed following a public outcry after the notorious Bentley/Craig murder case, when Christopher Craig, who was only sixteen at the time, shot dead a policeman and was imprisoned whilst Derek Bailey, his co-defendant, who had been unarmed, was hanged.

Mr Baker commented that Parliament had passed an Act which provided that only in certain cases of murder should the death penalty remain, one of those cases is murder in the furtherance of theft and this was what was charged here he said. Mr Baker went on to tell the jury that the prosecution did not know who had struck the fatal blow because each defendant blamed the other. He went on to say that Gus Roberts's skull had been fractured. There were several cut wounds caused by an iron bar and other marks on a forearm, which indicated that he had put up a considerable struggle.

In a statement to the police Mitchell said 'I went to grab the money tin but Gussie went to grab it off me, then George Jones hit Gussie with the bar and I ran out of the shop with the tin.' However, Jones denied this and said 'It's a pack of lies, Mitchell went into the back room, I heard a scuffle and Gus moaning saying 'Don't do it.'

The robbery was stupid, inept, unsophisticated and needless...an old man killed for £8 or £9 pounds. After their getaway, Mitchell went to a relative's house and produced £2 worth of small change which he told them he had won it playing cards with Jones. He went to the *Ivy Bush* public house in Clarence Place and paid for several drinks with loose change, he also asked for a £1 note and a 10 shilling note for more small change, 'You must have robbed a gas meter' said the barmaid. Jones later went to a tobacconist and asked for £2 in exchange for coins. These details were reported by Mr George Baker for the prosecution. At the close of the statement on behalf of the prosecution, Mr Alan King Hamilton submitted to Mr Justice Elwes that if the Crown did not know which of the two men had killed Gus Roberts, then the jury could not possibly know and that leaving that decision to them was tantamount to asking them to guess. He asked the judge to direct that the jury should acquit both accused on the Capital Murder charge. To his surprise the judge did not agree and the trial continued.

In the witness box, Jones described himself as a labourer and said that he had lost the sight of his right eye when he was twelve years old. He informed the court that he had obtained his trousers, overcoat vest and pullover from a dustbin and was given a jacket by the WVS (Women's Voluntary Service). He and Mitchell had gone to the Old Town Dock where Mitchell had picked an iron bar, which he had placed inside his coat. Jones admitted going to the paper shop but added 'I never touched the man. My conscience is clear, I never took anything from the shop.' In cross examination he denied handling the iron bar and said that Mitchell reached for the tin containing the money when Gus Roberts stood up to protest. He went on to say that Mitchell caught hold of Roberts by the neck and then pulled out the iron bar. 'I seen him strike twice,' said Jones.

When Mitchell, who was married with two children, gave evidence he said he had drunk six or seven pints of beer and was 'pretty drunk.' He met with Jones and agreed to get hold of some money. Mitchell said that he had used the iron bar to open up the shop door, but had then handed the bar to Jones. 'I went into the little room at the back of the shop to grab the money tin. Roberts got hold of it as well and some of the money spilled out. I saw Jones with the bar in his hand.' He denied striking Roberts or using any form of violence, at the end of his lengthy evidence, Mitchell said that he did not actually see Jones strike any blow.

Mr Ryder Richardson, defending Jones, described Mitchell as a dominant, purposeful and brutal man who was determined to stick to his story, Jones, however was a weak man and a simple thinker. Mr Alan King Hamilton, representing Mitchell said on his own admission that Mitchell was a thief but that did not make him a murderer. The prosecution had not proved their case and Gus Roberts' death would not be avenged by the hanging of an innocent man.

There were two moments of high drama whilst the accused were giving evidence in the witness box. The first when Mitchell was handed the iron bar by his defending counsel and was asked to demonstrate, how according to his evidence Jones had used it. Those people sitting on the press bench had to duck when Mitchell raised the bar in both hands, swinging it in their direction he shouted 'Jones had it like this Sir.' Secondly, after Jones had denied striking the killer blows he lost his temper and exclaimed 'I never touched the man.' He threw his hands into the air and tried to leave the witness box. A police officer held him back and the Judge warned Jones to control himself.

In his summing up Mr Justice Elwes directed the jury that under the Homicide Act it was open to convict one man of Capital Murder and if they were uncertain who had struck the fatal blows they were to convict both men of Non-Capital Murder.

After a two-hour retirement the jury returned at 7 pm to find both men guilty of Non-Capital Murder. They were jailed for life and thus a new chapter in British legal history began.

CHAPTER 18

You Always Hurt the One You Love
1965

What he discovered was appalling.

In the summer of 1965, a sixteen-year-old girl called Carol Brend, who lived on Caerleon Road, Newport, took a walk with her boyfriend, nineteen-year-old Colin Murdoch who lived in the same area. Carol was about to take the final walk of her short life.

Colin and Carol had been going out together for about six months when the horrific murder happened in July 1965. Colin, who lived in Collier Street, Newport, went to Carol's home to invite her, a female friend, and a younger boy on a walk in a nearby timber yard, but only Carol and Colin went. They set off with their arms around each other, a picture of young love. Half an hour later Colin Murdoch was seen climbing over the timber yard gate, and he appeared to be wild and exited. That evening Murdoch went to Maindee Police Station with a couple of friends. He was very upset, and kept saying that he had injured his girlfriend. His distress was obvious and the issue by now had made him desperate and uncontrollable. He needed to be restrained at one point so that

Part of the timber yard in Crawford Street, Newport, where the body of sixteen-year-old Carol Brand was found in 1965.

the facts could be established.

Ex-Detective Sergeant Doug Baker, was upstairs in the station at the time and hearing the commotion, went downstairs to see what was going on. After talking to Murdoch, Sergeant Baker went out to look for the girlfriend and to see what had happened. What he discovered was appalling. Sergeant Baker found the bloodstained body of the sixteen-year-old girl, Carol Brend. Her body lay at the rear of Crawford Street, just off Caerleon Road. Sergeant Baker went back to Maindee police station and charged Murdoch with her murder.

Mr Charles Lawson, QC prosecuting said that after Carol Brend left home to go for a walk, Murdoch was seen climbing over the timber yard gate, he seemed to be out of control and when questioned by the police, the defendant had informed them that he had hit her about the head, then asked a friend to go to the police station with him. Mr Lawson alleged Murdoch said, 'She was keeping on and on so I hit her.' He said they went to Maindee police station, where Murdoch had walked straight through to a writing room at the back.

When the police found the body, under Murdoch's direction, he had asked them if she was all right, said Mr Lawson. He then told the police, 'She was always on to me to do things, she asked for it.' Later he said 'I hit her and hit her with a piece of wood.' And then he broke down in tears. Lawson explained what a difficult and unpleasant job it had been for the police, especially for the officer charged with the job of informing the family of Carol's death. He described the case as tragic and said it had shocked the local community. Both Carol Brend and Colin Murdoch were from good families, which made the incident even harder to understand.

The court was told that a few weeks after Carol's death, her father, Mr Frederick Brand, received a letter from Murdoch, in it he was said to have apologised for all the trouble he had caused the family 'after your kindness and the way you treated me.' It went on 'Your daughter Carol meant everything to me, after what I have done to her, I don't care what happens to me, I have ruined my life, and whatever I get for this is not enough for what I have done.' Murdoch, after being sentenced to life in prison for murder, was subsequently released from prison to kill again.

Colin Murdoch gave himself up to police after stabbing his wife to death – just as he had done twenty-five years earlier when he had walked into a Newport Police Station. On that occasion, in 1965, he had told the police that he had injured his girlfriend, and shortly afterwards the police found her body. After his second killing, Murdoch left his wife's body on their bedroom floor and then led three of their children to the local police station where, once again, he gave himself up.

In Bristol Crown Court, standing between his two daughters and his son, one still dressed in pyjamas, Murdoch admitted manslaughter on the grounds of diminished responsibility. 'I have murdered my wife, she hit me, and I stabbed her again and again.'

Murdoch was then aged forty-five, and was now living on Smythe Road, Ashton, Bristol. He was sentenced to life imprisonment for the manslaughter of his wife, Angela. The Court was told that Angela, a secretary, who had a child by another man, knew about Murdoch's past life when she met him. Despite this, the relationship flourished, and in the six years of marriage they had had three children of their own.

Michael Hubbard, QC, prosecuting, said their relationship began to deteriorate when his wife developed a platonic friendship with a male work colleague. The couple agreed on a trial separation, but on the night of the murder, 'devoted husband', Murdoch returned to the home and began rowing with Angela. In a fit of rage, Murdoch handed Angela a hunting knife and begged her to stab him. When she refused, he plunged the blade into her chest ten times, piercing her heart three times.

Sentencing him, Mr Justice Hutchison said 'This is the second time you have killed a person you loved. In these circumstances one cannot but feel the greatest disquiet as to the risks you impose to the community – not the community at large – but to anybody with whom you develop an intimate relationship.' There was no option but to sentence Colin Murdoch to life in prison.

CHAPTER 19

Concern for a Missing Woman
1971

*Mr Yafai was seen throwing small bloodstained parcels
into the furnace...*

In Grafton Road, Newport, there is a small row of pleasant houses just a stone's throw from the main gate leading into the Newport Athletic Grounds, home of Newport Rugby Club. Most Saturdays thousands of people pass by a quiet house without knowing what happened there on Thursday, 2 September 1971.

Mrs Mary Yafai and her husband, Mr Yafai, and four children, Ablah, aged twelve, Ismahan, aged eleven, Yasmin, who was eight, and Muna, aged seven, lived happily in their home and fitted well into the community. Mary Yafai had time for everyone. Her husband, Ali, worked at the Llanwern Steel Works and was kept busy at home or maintaining his job to support his family with a good standard of life.

Hicks' (Funeral Directors) is situated just a few houses away from the house that Mrs Mary Yafai disappeared from in 1971. Her body was never found.

Grafton Road, Newport, a small row of pleasant houses where Mrs Yafai lived in 1971.

On Saturday, 2 September, everything was about to change. We are told that Mary walked out of her home at 2 pm on that day after a domestic dispute with her husband. Apparently she was made distraught by the argument. Ali thought that Mary would contact him within a day or two, perhaps from her relative's home in Birmingham, but he heard nothing.

Mr Yafai, who was a native of the Yemen, hoped to enlist the help of the Arab communities in Birmingham, Manchester, Liverpool, Sheffield and South Sheilds in his bid to discover where his wife had gone. After a week had passed, he had heard nothing. At this time, Newport police were informed of Mary's disappearance.

A senior CID officer at Newport's Civic Centre HQ told the *South Wales Argus* that because of the length of time in which Mrs Yafai had failed to contact her family, concern for her safety was mounting. She had now been gone for eight days. 'We are concerned that she has not tried to get in touch with her husband, Mr Ali Yafai, or her children and other members of her family. It is fair to say that Mrs Yafai would have been distraught when she left the house after a family quarrel.'

On 15 September, Newport CID issued a photograph of the woman who had been missing from her home for nearly two weeks. Police issued a fresh appeal for information about Mrs Yafai, together with the photograph: 'We have one reported sighting in the South of England, but so far this sighting is unconfirmed. We would still appreciate any information from the public as to her whereabouts.' The police added, 'Mrs Yafai is described as 5 foot, 5 inches. tall, of stocky build, with a fresh complexion, long dark hair, round face and hazel eyes. She is believed to be wearing navy blue slacks and a white cardigan or jumper.

November 25th was Yasmin's birthday, she was nine years old, but when the postman called to the family's home in Grafton Road, Newport, one very important birthday message was missing. Yasmin's mother did not send a card, it had now been three months since she had disappeared, since then there had been more tears than laughter at the family's neatly painted home. Yasmin's father, her three sisters, and the police, hoped that today would bring a card or letter from Mrs Yafai but there was nothing. 'I thought today was the day when something would happen' Mr Yafai said disappointedly. 'I was worked up last night, thinking that today would bring an answer to it all. Yasmin has had cards from everywhere and a lot of presents – except from my wife.'

Every new alleged sighting of Mrs Yafai brought new hope to Yasmin and her sisters. The children used to cry for their mother and still asked and worried about her. Mr Yafai said, 'I promise my wife that if she gets in touch with me I will not stop her from doing what she wants, but if only she would just telephone the police or contact Yasmin to let us know she is alright.'

The head of Newport CID, Detective Chief-Inspector Jack Harries said, 'We hoped there would be some message from Mrs Yafai, we hoped this would be a sort of red letter day for the mother and that she would get in touch, if only to wish the child a Happy Birthday, but it appears she has not done so.' He added that the police were still keeping an open mind on the case, saying 'We would again appeal to anyone who can assist us in tracing Mrs Yafai to contact the police.'

The headlines on 2 December 1971 read:

MR YALFAI'S PILGRIMAGE TO TRACE HIS WIFE

Steelworker, Ali Yafai, plans to set out this weekend on a pilgrimage of hope to the big industrial centre of the midlands and the North of England. His wife disappeared from the family home in Newport three months ago and despite a nationwide appeal by the police, she has not been traced. Mr Yafai, who is a native of The Yemen, hopes to enlist the help of the Arab communities of the northern towns and cities in his bid to solve the mystery. His tour of the northern towns and cities will take several days, but he will be helped by members of the Yemen Workers Union, an organisation that represents the interests of his countrymen in Britain. He plans to visit nightclubs and restaurants armed with posters bearing a picture and description of his wife. The poster has been distributed to police forces throughout Britain. Mr Yafai said, 'I believe my wife is still alive, but I am worried and want to prove this to the police, my friends and my wife's family. I hope something comes of this, I cannot have this thing around my neck all the time.' Whilst he is away from Newport, friends of the family will look after the four Yafai children. The pilgrimage will go ahead with the blessing of the police. Detective Chief-Inspector, Jack Harries, Head of Newport's CID who has played a major role in the enquiries into Mrs Yafai's disappearance said, 'We have no objection to this, and if anything comes of it we will be pleased, of course.'

As the months went by with no news of Mrs Yafai, and no new developments from Mr Yafai's trip to the north of England, the police started to make inquiries nearer to home. Suspicion fell on Mr Yafai and the police suggested that he and his family should temporarily vacate their home, so that the police could make a thorough search of the property. This was agreed upon and Mr Yafai and his family moved out. At the same time police interviewed a number of workers from Llanwern Steel Works. A number of employees stated that on several occasions, Mr Yafai was seen throwing small, bloodstained parcels into the furnace, and when asked 'What's in the parcels?' he replied, 'My brother is a butcher, and some of his meat has gone bad, this is the best place for it.'

Meanwhile the police at Grafton Road were pulling up the carpets in the downstairs rooms. There they discovered bloodstained patches on the underside of the carpets; this prompted them to remove the floorboards. The scene under the floorboards was most revealing as quite a large quantity of dried blood could be seen together with other items. Yafai was immediately arrested and after some considerable time of being questioned, he was cautioned and charged with the murder of his wife, Mrs Mary Yafai, on or about 2 September 1971.

The case went to trial; Yafai told the court that his wife was having an affair with a man named Phillips. An attempt was made to trace the man, but he was never found. Yafai admitted his guilt. The Judge said that the crime was a terrible case of injustice, there didn't appear to be a 'Mr Phillips' and with the absence of a body, the only sentence he could pass was that of manslaughter. Mr Ali Yafai was given six years imprisonment. He left the court in tears.

CHAPTER 20

Double Killing in Blaenavon
1972

The scene inside the living room was horrendous...

Alifetime friendship came to a sudden end on Monday, 3 April 1972 in the town of Blaenavon, a quiet place, a few miles outside of Newport. Two men, seventy-seven-year-old Mr Isaac Hughes and lifelong friend, Mr James Arthur Waite, aged fifty, were savagely battered to death in the living room of Mr Hughes terraced house at Rifle Green, Blaenavon. Mr Waite was a miner, who once worked as a refuse collector with the Blaenavon Council, had been a close friend of Isaac Hughes for many years. They usually spent the nights drinking together, and always finished up at the *Rifleman's Arms*, which was about 100 yards away from where Mr Hughes lived. Mr Waite often stayed overnight with Mr Hughes, to save walking to own home at Victoria Row, a mile away across the mountainside.

Police investigating the murders, believed that the answer to the mystery lay somewhere in the town. Evidence indicated that it was possible that they were looking for two murderers, rather than one, as it seemed unlikely that an individual could

In April 1972 two men were found murdered just 100 yards from their local pub, the Rifleman's Arms, *in a terraced house in Rifle Green.*

The scene today at Rifle Green, where in 1972 two men, James Waite and Isaac Hughes were savagely battered to death. The house has since been demolished.

have done so much harm alone. Detectives and uniformed men, some with tracker dogs, had been drafted into Blaenavon from all parts of Monmouthshire. The hunt was concentrated on the vicinity of the house at Rifle Green, where the bodies were found to start with, then extended until the whole town had been systematically combed.

It was expected to take several days until everyone in Blaenavon had been interviewed. The police were trying to establish a motive for the killings. It could have been a robbery, but there was no evidence at that time that anything had been stolen from the house. They also wanted to trace the murder weapon that was believed to be a sharp instrument, probably made of metal, with a triangular head. Two men had walked with Mr Hughes and Mr Waite from the inn on the Monday night and the police had already interviewed them.

The scene inside the living room was horrendous, with both men savagely battered to death. Their bodies were covered with blood, one with still in the armchair and the other on the floor. There were bloodstains everywhere. Mr Hughes's brother, who had broken a window to gain entry, made the discovery. It was about 4.20 on 3 April when the two men were found. The murder weapon was struck with such force that it left indentations in their skulls. It was imperative that the weapon be recovered.

The police set up a mobile investigation headquarters outside Blaenavon police station. In the house to house enquiries, householders around Rifle Green were asked whether they knew either of the dead men, and when they last saw them. They were also asked if they were in the *Rifleman's Arms* on Easter Monday night, and who else could they recollect being on the premises that night. The police were trying to trace a dull red van, driven by an Irishman, who had stayed the night at Mr Hughes's house on Good Friday. The Irishman was accompanied by his wife and two children, and was believed to have met Mr Hughes in the *Rifleman's Arms* on Good Friday night. He had paid him for a night's lodgings, when they left on the Saturday morning they said that they were heading for Crickhowell.

Mr Hughes farmed a smallholding at Llanellen, near Abergavenny, until he had retired ten years earlier. He lived in a caravan until about six weeks before he bought the house at Rifle Green. He paid £300 for the property and moved in.

Although police described him as a bachelor, it was discovered that he had been married, but that he had been separated from his wife for about thirty years. The motive for the crime had not been determined with any certainty. Money may have been taken from the house, but they were not certain at that stage.

A man and a nineteen-year-old blonde, who had been assisting the police with their enquiries, were both cleared from the case. The man, aged twenty, and the woman were allowed to leave the murder hunt headquarters after being interviewed. The couple had been seen at the *Rifleman's Arms* on Easter Monday night, shortly before the two men were battered to death. The police issued a description of the couple, and a photo-fit picture of the man. They were traced to Romford, in Essex, and had returned to Blaenavon with police officers who went to Romford to collect them. They spent more than five hours at the murder hunt headquarters. The pair were on a hitch-hiking holiday in South Wales, and had called at the *Rifleman's Arms* as they were passing through Blaenavon.

The police were now concentrating on a search for a man in a black overcoat and trilby hat, who had been seen loitering

Police search the ground outside the house at Blaenavon.

near the scene of the crime. A description of the man, who had been seen by four people, was issued the following weekend.

The police were also continuing with systematic searches of the area, in the hope of finding the murder weapon, and were still appealing to the public for information. The Irishman with the red van, whom the police believed could assist with their investigation, was traced in London. Gwent police went to London on the Saturday and returned with the family and two other Irishmen, believed to be the man's brothers. After being interviewed, they returned to London without being charged.

Colonel Kenneth Treasure, the Monmouthshire coroner, made an appeal for public co-operation in solving the double murder. When he opened the inquest on the two murdered men at Pontypool, he said:

> An appeal has been made by the police to the public and particularly the people of Blaenavon, to co-operate with them, and come forward with any information that would bring to a close to this horrendous crime. I would like to re-enforce the appeal and urge any member of the public, if they have any information, of any kind, although they may not themselves consider it of any great importance, to go to the police at once. Any piece of assistance the police get, in a case of this kind, should be made available to them.

Formal evidence of identification was given by Mr Charles Henry Hughes, the brother of Mr Hughes. He said that his brother was married, but living apart from his wife. He moved to Rifle Green in February 1972, having previously lived in a caravan. He was very friendly with Mr Waite, for several years they had been drinking pals and used to go out together. It was not unknown for Mr Waite to spend the night with Mr Hughes, particularly at weekends. Mr Hughes told the coroner, 'I never heard my brother express any intention of doing anything to himself or any other person. He was a placid, quiet man, friendly and kind to everyone.'

In the case of Mr Waite, a brother, Mr Dan Albert Waite, of Blaenavon, gave evidence of identification. He confirmed that his brother had been very friendly with Mr Hughes. His brother enjoyed good health and he had last seen him about lunchtime on Easter Monday. 'I was accompanied by my wife, I saw him coming from the *Old Rock and Fountain* and going to the *Rifleman's Arms*. He was some distance away.' He said, 'My brother was normally in good spirits, and was a man who enjoyed life.' He added, 'I never heard him say anything to the effect that he was fed up. He enjoyed life; he liked a drink, but never did any harm to anyone. He was well thought of.'

The man in black never came forward. On 8 April, Superintendent V J Shortridge said, 'we badly need information, the police are intensifying their hunt for the murderer, and house-to-house enquiries continued today. To date, more than 2,500 people have been interviewed, it is our intention to go ahead, until such time as we have interviewed every responsible adult in the community.'

Thirty-two years later 'The Easter Monday Killings' remain unsolved.

CHAPTER 21

The Malpas Murder
1988

... Danny could not have known the horror that was to follow.

Monday morning, 18 January 1988, Danny Denbury left his Newport home at Malpas and made his way to the town centre. He was a well-respected member of the community, a gentleman who had time for everyone. At around 10 o'clock on this Monday morning, Danny paid a visit to a neighbour who lived in Pillmawr Road, a regular social call that he made every day. He then left and started his morning walk to town, not knowing that every step he took was one step closer to death.

Leaving behind him the respectability of the Malpas community, in which he lived, he continued towards the town's twighlight homosexual world, in which he had become so well known. At midday he was seen walking past the *Three Horseshoes* public house, in the direction of Malpas Road. Danny later arrived at Newport town centre and headed for some of his favourite haunts. Whatever his thoughts were as he headed for the town, we shall never know, but Danny could not have known the horror of what was to follow.

On 19 January, at about 11.30 am, neighbours noticed that Danny's milk was still on the doorstep, and they were worried that something was wrong. The neighbours contacted Danny's brother, Neil Denbury, who came to the house and went upstairs, where he found his brother's body.

Newport police were called, and one of the biggest murder investigations ever seen in Gwent was under way. Danny's home was immaculate, but the room where his brother had found him was now a blood bath. His face had been severely battered, and his hands and feet were tied before he was clubbed to death. He had died, choking on his own blood when his face was smashed in. Police believed that Danny had been left alive, but that he had died some time later. Money was missing from the house and some items of Danny's clothing were also missing.

The quiet gentleman of Pillmawr Road, Malpas, Newport, would be remembered for many years to follow, by friends and relatives as a man, who by nature, should not have had an enemy in the world. He was a home loving bachelor who 'kept himself to himself' but was always pleasant and friendly. Aged sixty-two, Danny had never married, but he shared the home of an old friend, Sam Price. Danny moved in with Sam when Mrs Price had died.

Danny made regular visits to a number of lonely people who lived in his area and was always willing to help them with their problems. He worked for Standard Telephones and Cables for over thirty years and was well liked by the workforce. Danny loved his trips to the town centre, and was well known in many of Newport's pubs and bars. The last times that people recalled seeing him was at 1 pm on 18 January, going into the *Sovereign Bar*. At 1.35 pm he was seen in Commercial Street, outside British Home Stores. He was chatting to someone until 1.55 pm. He told them he was meeting a friend at 2.10 pm. Danny arrived at *Oscar's Bar* alone. He was next seen at the *Albert Hotel*, which he left at 2.20 pm. Next, he arrived at *Jekyll and Hyde's Bar* at about 2.40 in the *Westgate Hotel*. Now he was seen in the company of another man. The two men sat down, chatted and drank together, Danny bought the drinks. His companion seemed to be very polite. At 3 o'clock they had their last drink, and they left together shortly afterwards. There was now a mystery. At about the time that they were in the bar, a man phoned a Newport taxi firm to order a cab for Danny. The voice was rather gruff, not the voice of Danny. Most taxi firms knew Danny, so they must have assumed that someone rang for him. When the taxi driver turned out to pick up Danny at the requested location, he did not arrive. The driver waited for a time, and then left. At 3.15 pm, the two men were seen at Newport Bus Station. They got on the 3.20 pm Number 3 bus for Malpas.

At 4.00 o'clock the paperboy delivered the newspaper to Mr Denbury's house. The house appeared to be empty. Also, just after 4 pm, Danny and his drinking friend were seen walking along Pillmawr Road towards Danny's house. That was the last time that Danny Denbury was seen alive.

Police launched a massive murder hunt to find his killer. They confirmed that they were treating the death as murder and immediately set up an incident room at Maindee Police Station. The inquiry was headed by Gwent's top detective, Chief Superintendent Mark Waters. A press conference was organised, and the police appealed for anyone who may have seen him or visited his house, since Monday afternoon, 18 January. Anyone with information was told to contact the incident room, or any police station.

Unemployed Christopher Paul McGovern, the face of the man wanted on suspicion of the murder of Danny Denbury.

The *South Wales Argus* reported that many of Gwent's homosexual community might know the suspected murderer, but might be too afraid to reveal his identity to the police. This was also the theory of the detectives as it seemed likely that their suspect was a well-known importuner. It was noted that some homosexuals were reluctant to come forward, fearing the break-up of their regular relationship if they admitted knowing him.

Police quizzed one man who said he was offered sex by a man fitting the description of the key suspect, but the police leading the hunt said 'Many others must have known him and are afraid to come forward. All information will be treated in the strictest confidence, but they must hear from the suspect's sex partners.' Chief Superintendent Waters thought the suspect was believed to be an importuner that waited in public lavatories, in and around Newport. The man they were searching for was about forty-five years of age, of slim build, with a moustache. He had a distinctive high forehead and swept-back, old fashioned 'wet look' black hair, which could be dyed. It was possible that he had changed his appearance since the killing and was now staying away from the gay environment.

Mr Denbury was known to have met regularly with the suspect, and was seen on a number of occasions drinking with him in the *Albert Hotel*, Newport. Police were anxious to trace an auburn-haired man seen drinking with the two men in the *Albert* on a Saturday afternoon at the beginning of January. The *Argus* published an impression of the face the police wanted to interview in connection with the Denbury murder.

On Friday, 5 February 1988, murder hunt detectives from Newport's central police station questioned a man about the killing. He was twenty-eight, and had been arrested the night before after three dramatic police swoops on separate houses in and around Newport. No charges were made. Mark Waters, the Gwent CID boss, said that charges were expected later that day. In a brief statement, Mr Waters said the man was arrested between 6 pm and 6.30 pm on the previous night in a house in the Baneswell area of Newport. He revealed that police had gone to the house after receiving information.

Plain-clothed squads of police pounced on three houses between 5 pm and 6.30 pm on Thursday, 4 February, one in St Brides, between Newport and Cardiff, one at Commercial Road in the town centre and one at Baneswell. The man they were now interviewing was arrested at the Baneswell house by four police officers. Detective Constable Price, at the front door noticed someone behind the glass door doing some decorating. He placed his police badge against the glass, shouted out 'Police!' And pushed the door against the passage wall which trapped the decorator. The man caught between the glass door and the wall turned out to be Christopher Paul McGovern, who was arrested by Detective Sergeant Wyatt on suspicion of the murder of Danny Denbury. On being cautioned, McGovern is alleged to have replied, 'What murder, I don't know what you're talking about?' Later he denied knowing Danny Denbury. At the time of his arrest, McGovern was in the process of decorating the hallway of the address at Windsor Terrace and the arresting officers were fortunate to have been able to apprehend him swiftly and without any resistance. McGovern, was an unmarried, unemployed, ex soldier who came originally from Manchester, he had been living in various parts of Newport for the past eighteen months.

Mr Denbury was last seen alive the on 7 January when he went drinking in a number of Newport town centre pubs. Police were later able to trace his movements in the town centre and his bus ride back to Malpas. He was last seen going into his home at 4 pm that afternoon. On Saturday, 6 February 1988, a twenty-eight-year-old man appeared before Newport Magistrates' Court, charged with the murder of Danny Denbury, on or about 18 January.

Unemployed, Christopher Paul McGovern, who gave his address as Windsor Terrace, Baneswell, Newport, but was described as having no fixed address, was remanded in custody to Cardiff prison until the following week. There was no application for bail, and legal aid was granted. The following week magistrates remanded McGovern in custody for a further seven days, but McGovern chose not to appear before the court until 8 April.

In court, the alleged killer, Christopher McGovern, denied that a mystery man at Danny Denbury's home was a figment of his imagination. He also denied that it was he who murdered Mr Denbury in a cool and calculated killing. He had not told 'persistent lies' to cover up the brutal attack, and that he had not attacked a defenceless old man leaving him to die a horrible death. McGovern also claimed he did not contact the police because he panicked when he saw a circulated photo fit picture of a wanted man with a similar hairstyle to his own. The denials were told to a jury at Newport Crown Court by the head of Gwent's CID on the fourth day of McGovern's trial.

Detective Chief Superintendent Mark Waters, told the court that McGovern had told him he went with Mr Denbury to his home to borrow some pornographic books. When they arrived another man, called John, was already there. McGovern said he left when Mr Denbury and the other man began having sex. McGovern insisted that he had not killed Danny Denbury. Asked why he had not come forward, following publicity about the murder, McGovern said he had panicked when he saw photo fit pictures of a suspect.

Eventually, Christopher McGovern admitted and confessed to having murdered Danny Denbury. His motive was that he wanted to watch the older man die for 'trying it on': he did not like Danny Denbury making gay sexual advances towards him. It is claimed he admitted stabbing Denbury with a potato peeler and beating him repeatedly.

The alleged confession was told to the jury at Newport Crown Court by Anthony James, of Cardiff Road, Newport, during the McGovern trial. Mr James said he was a fellow prisoner at Cardiff prison in February when McGovern was there on remand. Mr James, who had now completed his sentence for burglary said that the conversation had taken place in the prison's hospital wing, where both men were working. He said that he asked McGovern if he had killed Mr Denbury and he replied 'yes', asked why, and he said Mr Denbury had tried it on in the kitchen. 'He said he stabbed him with a potato peeler, dragged him into the lounge and beat him repeatedly with his fists, feet and the potato peeler.' He said 'I wanted to see him die for what he had done.'

McGovern swore at his former fiancé, a nurse, in an outburst from the dock. As the nurse gave evidence he shouted 'You are a lying bastard you are.' The ex-fiancée of the alleged killer denied that she was lying to the jury just to 'make matters worse for him.' She said that she no longer liked the man she had lived with for nearly two years. She said that she no longer had contact with him. She then told the court that McGovern returned home with red, stained clothing the day Danny Denbury died. She told the court that he had arrived home about three hours later than the time he allegedly told the police. She had washed his stained jeans and jacket in the early hours of the morning. Apparently he had returned to their flat three hours later than the time that he had told the police. This would have been at 8.50 pm. McGovern had told her that the stains were red oxide from his work.

The jury was then told by Mr John Griffith Williams, prosecuting, that McGovern was 'living a lie' and that he did not have a job. He also told the police that he went to Mr Denbury's home and stole his wallet containing about £100, and then had left him there with another man. The prosecution said that an electrical alarm clock at Mr Denbury's home had stopped at 7.50 pm. Its flex was cut and used to tie up Mr Denbury.

The ex-soldier charged with killing Danny Denbury was not a homosexual-hater, his defence counsel said. The brutal killer was finally trapped by an unpaid hotel bill. On Sunday, 21 June 1987, Christopher Paul McGovern was arrested for leaving a hotel in Monmouth without paying his bill. After staying there from 11 April to the 21st. As a result of the charge that followed, he was fingerprinted. After Mr Denbury's death, part of the murder investigation included a police operation to check fingerprints found in the house. This was an exhaustive enquiry, which involved eliminating everyone who had lawful access to the house. An unaccounted fingerprint was found near the murdered man's body. It was identified as McGovern's. Police arrested him and the fingerprint was later to provide one of a number of pieces of evidence against him.

Danny Denbury shouldn't have had any enemies, he was a home bird, he was placid, friendly, not aggressive in any way, and always very pleasant. He was well dressed, well mannered and well liked. The former soldier, Christopher Paul McGovern, was, on Wednesday, 14 December 1988, jailed for life by Newport Crown Court, after being found guilty by a unanimous jury. The verdict followed a marathon, eight-day hearing. McGovern had consistently denied killing sixty-two-year-old Mr Danny Denbury at his Malpas home, Newport, in January. It had taken the jury nearly four hours to unanimously find Paul McGovern guilty of his murder.

CHAPTER **22**

Body in the Bags Murder
1990

It... was the most sickening sight in his nine years as a policeman.

In the small village of Rogerstone, nothing much seems to happen, but this all changed on 21 March 1990. Rogerstone, just a few miles from Newport, the A467 bypass, and a busy road that runs from Newport to Risca and on to Abertillery, is hardly ever without fast moving traffic. But this all changed on Wednesday, 21 March when two bags were seen lying on a small roadside bank at 7.30 in the morning. At that time no one had time to stop to investigate, most vehicle drivers were either off to work and in a hurry, or

The scene of the Rogerstone bypass where on 21 March 1990, two bags were found on the side of a very busy main road. Each bag contained parts of a human body.

On 25 March 1990, a red bag was found near Orchard Farm at St Brides, by a farm worker. It contained the head and hands of murder victim Clive Tully, a visitor to this country from New Zealand.

making the first delivery of the day for the company that they worked for. Some of the regular users of the by-pass road noticed the bags were not there the day before, so contact with the local police was established.

The police arrived at the scene, which seemed like another case of rubbish dumping. It was near lunchtime that PC Jeff Harris, stationed at Rogerstone, unzipped both bags and raised the alarm when he discovered parts of a human body inside. It turned out to be the most sickening sight in his nine years as a policeman. 'I have dealt with sudden death before but I have never seen anything as gruesome.' PC Harris was reacting to a call from a member of the public, which alerted police to the fact that the two bags had apparently been abandoned by the side of the road.

When he opened the first bag he found inside a number of smaller bags wrapped in polythene. In the second bag he found just one large bag. On opening the parcel, almost immediately he realised that he was looking at parts of a human body. The nearest thing to human skin is pig, but he knew that was not the case, the texture was different and the amount of hair was totally different to that of a pig.

PC Harris called for help for a second opinion and had his worst fears confirmed by his Chief Inspector. The headless and handless body had been carefully sliced in two, the naked torso, arms and legs of the butchered man were found divided between the two bags. The head and hands were missing in an attempt to avoid the man's identification.

A full-scale murder hunt was launched involving thirty officers and there was a national alert. Gwent CID boss, Chief Superintendent Mark Waters said, 'I am desperate to identify the man.' Police also wanted to trace the source of the bags, which could have been bought specifically to put the body inside.

A hotline was set up and a murder incident room at Maindee Police Station, Newport. Detectives revealed details of clothing, which could provide vital clues in the headless corpse murder hunt. There was a blue woollen sweater with a V-neck, size 40-inch chest. The label read 'John Barry Knitwear, Made in England.' Details of the rucksack and holdall which held the man's remains were as follows. The rucksack was black with red piping and bearing an outbound motif. It retailed at about £60 from a number of outlets, mainly camping and leisure shops. The holdall was maroon in colour. It was known that the dead man had put up a struggle because of some classic defence wounds. There would also have been a great deal of blood at the murder scene. Police believed the killing had happened in a house or a flat and urged people to think about the day the body was found, particularly the week-end before. Anyone who had heard a violent argument, a fight, or the sound of someone struggling out of a house or flat with heavy bags, then putting them into a vehicle was asked to come forward. In the days that followed, police visited youth hostels and issued photographs of the body. They also visited 'The Mountain Centre' at the Brecon Beacons, a well-known gathering point for travellers. The lists of people who had stayed there were checked.

On 25 March, Andrew Newbury, a farm worker, who was helping with the lambing at Orchard Farm, St Brides, saw a red bag as he drove a tractor along St Brides Road, Newport. The bag was in a roadside ditch. He went to investigate and found a round parcel inside. It was a football shaped object, wrapped in a clear plastic bag, fastened with tape and covered with a blood stained cloth. Mr Newbury put the bag back and took a few minutes to compose himself before the police were called.

Inside the cloth were the head and hands of the victim. Also other human remains, such as a nose and an ear. This second finding stunned the people of Newport. There were two questions to be answered. What was the motive for killing what was now known to be a young man, and why were the bags of body parts dumped on the side of roads? The first bags were left in a location, which would have been seen, by many drivers, and the second, in a fairly quiet road. Local people, from St Brides, used the road.

The news that shook the town made the front page of the *South Wales Argus* for several evenings. It was then decided to develop a computerised photograph of the mans face. The *Argus* Art Editor, Geoff Fowler was given the task, which he achieved by using the latest techniques. Once an image had been produced, it was published on the front page for several evenings in the hope that someone would recognise him.

The police received dozens of phone calls, naming quite a few people, but one name came to the top of the list. It was the name of a backpacker from Australia or New Zealand called 'Tully.' An *Argus* journalist who worked in the same building as the Art Editor, Geoff Fowler, by the name of Paul Tully, discovered that the victim was his cousin, Clive Tully. Clive, was in fact from New Zealand and had visited his cousin a few months earlier. Paul Tully met his cousin in the April. Clive had come to visit his long lost relatives whilst travelling around the world. Paul said, 'He was a normal, lively twenty-four-year-old, who had come over to meet relatives and get some work where he could.' He had apparently stayed in a hotel, but was thought to have left the country. 'He came over here to meet lost relatives and ended up being killed. All the family are stunned.'

The victim, Clive Tully.

Paul added 'Clive must have stayed in Britain because he enjoyed it so much.'

It was Paul's brother Geoff, who recognised Clive through the *Argus* computer reconstruction of the murder victim's face. *Argus* editor, Geoff Fowler took the police photograph of the dead man and made it look like a live man by removing bloodstains and facial injuries, and adding eyes from another *Argus* journalist with a similar shaped face. Ironically, it was the eyes that led to the identification; Geoff Tully saw the likeness of his cousin immediately. Information about the backpacker, Clive Tully, came to the Newport Police Headquarters from many parts of the country. People said they had met Clive on his tour of Great Britain.

Most of the calls came from Bristol, a Mr Michael Higgins, a site foreman from a Western-Super-Mare building company told the police that Clive Tully worked for them in 1989. Mr Tully gave in his notice after a disagreement over Christmas bonus pay. Mr Higgins said he fired Mr Tully in early January 1990 for not working properly after giving notice. Mr Tully then left for a tour of Spain and Portugal. Mr Higgins said that before he went, Mr Tully sold a bed from the house at Luxton Street, Bristol. Mr Higgins' parents owned the house, and the bed belonged to his sister. Mr Higgins told the police that he was very angry with this, and remembered saying that if he ever saw Tully again, he would kill him; but I did not mean it. Mr Tully returned from Spain and Portugal, to the flat in Luxton Street, Bristol. He had shared the flat with a Malcolm John Green.

A team of police officers went to the flat to investigate and discovered a trail of blood leading up the stairs at the alleged scene of the killing of Clive Tully. Spots of blood, which could have come from Tully, were found on twelve steps leading from the sitting room to the bathroom. Downstairs an attempt had been made to wash bloodstains from a carpet, Green denied murdering Mr Tully.

Forensic scientist Michael Rogers said that at Green's home he found bloodstains about four feet square on a downstairs carpet and whilst examining them he noticed a strong smell of soap, washing powder, or something similar. Michael Rogers said 'My impression was that there had been an attempt to wash blood from the carpet.' A blood smear was also found on a settee castor and on the underside of a table. The waste pipes and u-bends of the bath and hand basin gave a positive chemical reaction to blood, but it was impossible to say if it was human blood.

The prosecution alleged that Green murdered twenty-four-year-old Mr Tully at the house before dismembering him either in the sitting room or the bathroom. At the trial Mr Paul Chadd QC, prosecuting, said a finger print from Green was found on the plastic bag containing two forearms and also on the plastic bag wrapped around the head. The prosecution suggested that Green had rained a dozen blows on Clive Tully's head with something like a hammer, at the house where both men had lived in Luxton Street, Bristol. He then dismembered the body leaving a trail of 'bloody drips' in the house before driving to Newport to dump the bags. A motorist picked Green out of an identity parade as the man he saw place a holdall on the A467 at Rogerstone. Avon and Somerset police fingerprint expert Kenneth Hobbs told the court that fingerprints from Green were among the prints found on each of the two plastic bags containing body parts, therefore Green was guilty of murder. Green is alleged to have told the police that when Mr Tully returned from Spain and Portugal, Tully went to see him and said he had no money and wanted somewhere to stay. Green said he had lent him £50, after they had a cup of coffee together, he left Mr Tully and went to his girlfriend's house, and that he did not see Mr Tully again, saying 'I did not murder Tully, I know nothing about it, I am being set up.'

At the trial in October and November 1991, at Bristol Crown Court, Malcolm John Green, aged forty-three, of Luxton Street, Bristol, was found guilty of the murder of Clive Tully, a bagpacker from New Zealand. The Judge sentenced Green to life in prison. Questions were being tabled to the Home Secretary, Kenneth Baker, about reports that a psychiatrist had urged that Green should not be freed into the community because of his mental state.

It was five months after his release from a life sentence for the brutal killing of a Cardiff prostitute, that Green battered to death and butchered, Clive Tully. Home Secretary Baker said, 'This should never, never, happen again.' Clive Tully's family also demanded an inquiry why Green had been freed from his previous life sentence. They said he should never be allowed back into the community and believed if he was allowed to be released, whatever his age, he would kill again.

Whilst sentencing to life in prison, the Judge said he would recommend to the Home Secretary, that Green serve at least twenty-five years. As sentence was being passed, Green interrupted twice, saying, 'I did not kill Clive Tully.' When he was being led away, he turned to the public gallery and shouted 'THEY ARE WRONG!' Green was then taken away to begin life in prison.

Malcolm Green.

CHAPTER 23

The Lady Vanishes
1997

Gwent police began a missing persons investigation...

Michael Bowen lived in the Caldicot area, a few miles from Newport, and attended Caldicot Comprehensive, filled with ambition. At the age of seventeen, he left school and started work at several types of jobs until he found his niche in life. He spent most of his working life as a forestry worker in Wentwood, on the outskirts of Newport. This was the job he liked best.

He married at the age of twenty-two, but the marriage failed. Later he married his housekeeper, this relationship was stormy and also ended. In the early 1990s Michael took a job working on the Channel Tunnel in Kent. There he met a very attractive woman called Mrs Sandie King, who lived in the area. When the work on the tunnel was finished, Bowen and Mrs King

A row of lovely houses in the Wye Valley Village of Llandogo, near Chepstow, where Michael Bowen and his wife Sandie lived in 1997.

came back to live in Newport.

For a while Sandie King took a number of jobs by working in a guest house as a general housekeeper, as well as holding down a second job as a care assistant in a nursing home. Sandie was going through a divorce at this time. In November 1993 Sandie King and Michael Bowen married. They had been living together for fifteen months before the wedding. They were so much in love that they would leave sentimental notes for each other. Three years later the marriage began to deteriorate. Sandie's daughter, from her first marriage, noticed that her mother was unhappy.

In 1995, Michael and Sandie met the landlord who ran the local Sloop Inn, in the Wye Valley village of Llandogo. This was just a few miles from where the Bowen's now lived; they became friends and would often go fishing in the Wye river. By now Mrs Bowen was working in a pub at Llanmartin, and travelled there daily from Llandogo where the couple had recently moved. Michael Bowen was back as a forestry worker at Wentwood. Sandie then took a job as a caterer at the Llandogo function centre, Valley House, which was owned by their new-found friend. The two had become close friends, and later they began an affair.

In August 1997 Sandie decided to leave the couple's home at Hudnall's View, in the Wye Valley village of Llandogo. Afterwards Michael Bowen confronted Sandie about her adultery and told her he had started divorce proceedings. It was 5 August 1997, that friends and family last heard from Sandie. Anita Spencer, Sandie's daughter, tried time and time again to contact her mother, but she failed. Friends and neighbours knocked the door but there was no reply. On 8 August, Mrs Bowen failed to turn up for an appointment at the Royal Gwent Hospital, Newport. Anita Spencer reported that her mother was missing to the police in Kent. Gwent police began a missing person's investigation and started to make house-to-house enquiries.

On 10 August, police made a search of the couple's home in Llandogo. They found her medication, dentures and watch in a bin, also her passport and driving licence. In the following few days, hoteliers in Stratford-upon-Avon, claimed to have seen her. Her daughter, Anita, made an emotional appeal for information at a press conference. The search at Wentwood was widened to the woods at Trellech. A Newport florist said she saw Mrs Bowen on 6 August.

On 21 August 1997, Michael Bowen was charged with the murder of his wife. On 1 September, a specially trained dog searched the Wentwood reservoir. A massive search was made of the forest itself. Newport police were assisted by members of the public, but however, nothing was found. On 17 November, Bowen was given bail when his family put up a quarter of a million pounds surety. A police diving team was brought in to search the Wentwood reservoir for the second time, the divers were assisted by a dog that was trained to detect the gasses and micro-organisms given off by dead bodies under water. The cadaver dog used was called 'Milo' who was one of just seven such dogs in the country. Milo was also attached to the sub-aqua team of South Wales police force. Once again, nothing was found.

In May 1998 Bowen's trial took place at Newport Crown Court, Bowen denied murdering his wife Sandie; he also denied intimidating a witness. Patrick Harrington QC, defending, said that a Newport florist had told police officers she had seen a woman she believed to be Mrs Bowen on the day she disappeared. A closed-circuit television camera

How the murder was reported in the local press.

Murder shocked village

THE murder of Sandie Bowen shocked the quiet community of Llandogo and led to a ground-breaking police investigation.

Like the recent Jenna Baldwin case, police initially treated Sandie Bowen's disappearace as a missing person inquiry, but they were soon to realise they were looking at a murder investigation.

The 52-year-old mother and divorcee first met Michael Bowen in 1992, when the Wentwood forestry worker had been working on the Channel Tunnel in her home

MURDER PROBE: Police investigations at the Bowen home

was having an affair on the day she disappeared.

Just days after her disappearance, detectives suspected foul play, and found her glasses, make up and dentures in the dustbin.

Bowen was arrested and charged with his wife's murder on August 21, 1997.

After a five-week trial in May 1998, Bowen was convicted unanimously of his wife's murder by a jury at Newport crown court.

The prosecution case was very unusual in that evidence was purely circumstantial as there was no body.

situated outside of the shop would confirm the sighting. The court heard that the police had not looked at the footage. Mr Harrington also criticised the police for taking a month to interview two hoteliers in Stratford-upon-Avon, who claimed a woman they had met after the disappearance, was the same as the one in a newspaper appeal. He said that officers did not tell one of the proprietors, in whose hotel Mrs Bowen might have stayed, to seal off the room so that fingerprints could be taken.

Mr Harrington told Newport Crown Court, 'If he is guilty, he is a monster, because anyone who can kill rather than resort to the divorce courts has done something monstrous.' He then went on to say that Bowen was not a monster but a 'brilliant dad'. He also said that Mrs Bowen did not have a future. Her husband wanted to formally end their marriage, her daughter wanted to send her money but did not want her company, and a friend was no longer prepared to cover up her affair. In contrast, Michael Bowen had a future to look forward to with his new lover, whom he had planned to move in with.

David Aubrey QC prosecuting, said, 'Mrs Bowen was a woman who would not have just gone off without any contact with her family.'

Bowen had given evidence that his wife was shocked when he announced that he was getting a divorce, but Aubrey said that Mrs Bowen was already planning to leave their home at Hudnall's View, Llandogo. He said that some people who had killed and disposed of the body might be shaken, and show signs of it, but he added that Bowen was a callous individual, who had shown from the very beginning, that he did not have the slightest concern for his wife.

Mr Justice Eady, who had been hearing the case at Newport Crown Court, sent out the jury. The jury was due to resume its deliberations again the following morning. During his summing up, Mr Justice Eady told the jury that as a body had not been recovered, the prosecution's case was circumstantial. He added, 'There was no one to come forward to the court and say 'I saw this crime being committed'. He reminded the jury that three witnesses had said that they had seen Mrs Bowen after she had disappeared. If the jury thought it could have been Mrs Bowen, it would end the prosecution's case that Bowen had murdered his wife. Bowen had always claimed that in August 1997, Mrs Bowen had decided to leave the matrimonial home in Llandogo after he had confronted her about her adultery. He said that she had asked him to take her to Newport railway station, which he had done on 6 August, last. This was the last time he claimed to have seen her. Friends and family had last been in touch with Mrs Bowen the previous day, and none had seen or heard from her since.

The trial had been told Bowen was also having an affair with the wife of his fishing partner, which continued until December 1997. Bowen was charged with intimidating his former lover, a witness for the prosecution.

Where is my mother? This is the question Anita Spencer was asking after her stepfather, Michael Bowen, was jailed for life for murdering his wife, Sandie. Ms Spencer said, 'If anyone knows where she could be, I just hope they can tell me, I would like to find her body so that I could end it for my children and

I. Until I have a body and am able to put her to rest in a proper place, my life will never be the same.'

The police may interview Bowen in the future to see if they can establish where the body is of the lady that 'vanished'.

Sandie Bowen, the face that haunted the people of Newport and South Wales.

In 2004 Michael Bowen was taken to Newport Crown Court for a further judgement, hoping to obtain parole. He finally confessed to the murder of his wife, Sandie, but refused to say how he had committed the crime and where he had disposed of the body. His parole application was rejected.

Photo Gallery

The Odeon Cinema, Bristol where a former manager, Robert Parrington-Jackson was found murdered in his office, in 1946.

Robert Parrington-Jackson, former cinema manager of the 'Odeons' at Newport and Bristol.

The Charles Williams School, Caerleon, built in 1694. It bears the name of its illustrious founder (see Chapter 13: Till Death Us Do Part).

The Godfrey Morgan, Maindee Square, Newport, now a Witherspoon public house. It was formerly the Maindee Cinema, where George Jones went into hiding in 1959 (see Chapter 17: Sudden Death in Dock Street).

An oblique aeriel view of the Llanwern Steel Works, Newport, where several employees stated that Yafai was seen throwing small, bloodstained parcels into a furnace (see Chapter 19: Concern for a Missing Woman).

Index